# Build & Convert
# Classic British Jets

Compiled by Gary Hatcher

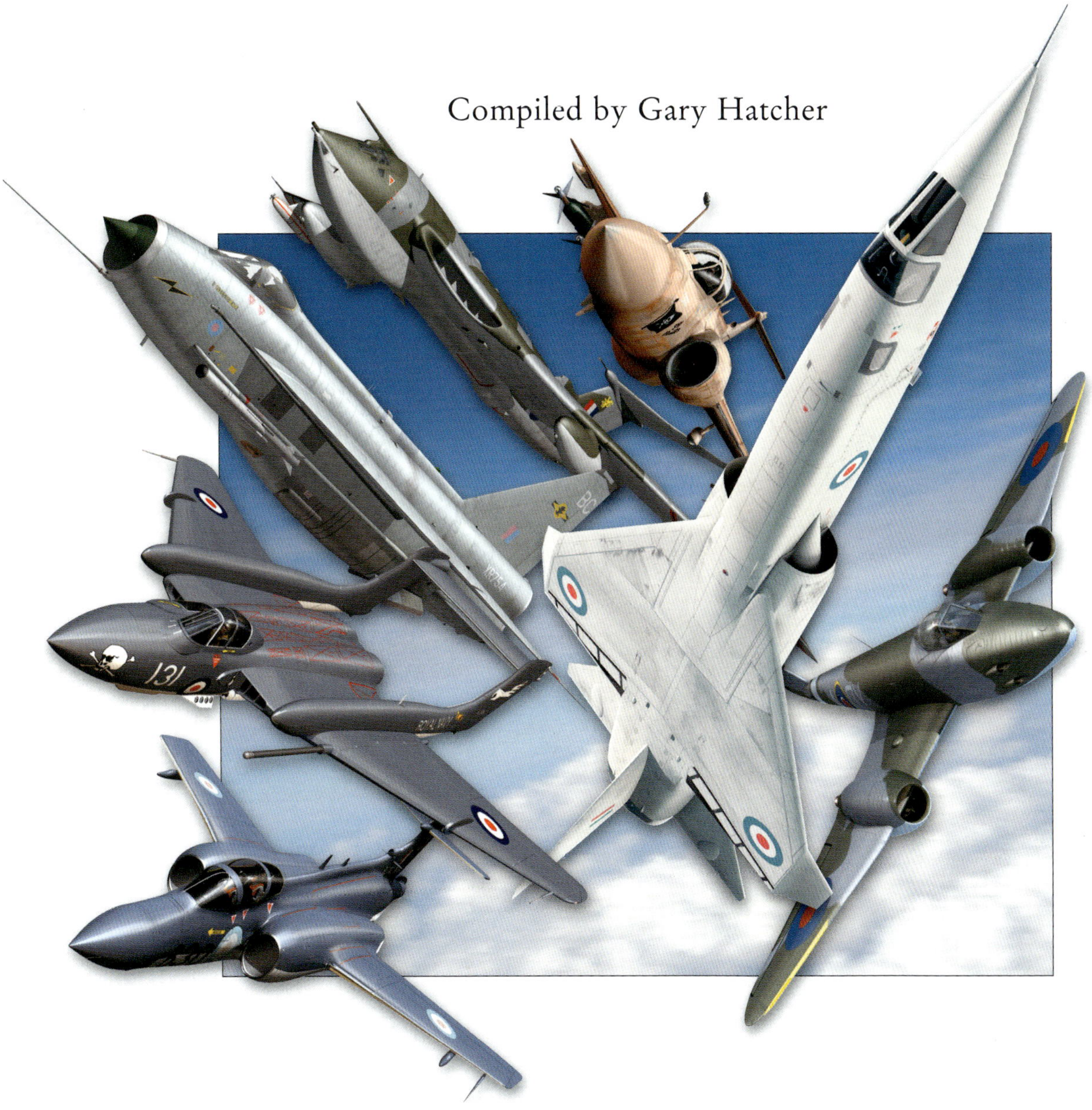

SAM PUBLICATIONS

**Cover Artwork courtesy of John Fox, Jerry Boucher and Hornby Hobbies Ltd.**

# Build and Convert 3
## Classic British Jets

Edited by Gary Hatcher

First produced in 2013 by Media House, under licence from SAM Publications

Media House, 21 Kingsway, Bedford, MK42 9BJ, United Kingdom

ISBN: 978-1-906959-28-9

Typeset by Media House, 21 Kingsway, Bedford, MK42 9BJ, United Kingdom

Designed by Jonathan Phillips

Printed and bound in the United Kingdom by Micropress Printers Ltd

This third volume in the series looks at modelling iconic British jet aircraft types with a selection of model builds and projects taken from the archives of *Scale Aviation Modeller International* and *Model Aircraft* magazines. Covering a variety of scales, techniques, and accessories, the features vary from quick out-of-the-box builds, to in-depth conversions and super-detailing.

Once again the book is endorsed by Airfix, and includes some of the best new toolings released by the resurgent company in recent years, including the Nimrod, the Canberra, the TSR 2 and the Valiant, as well as older kits from the range like the Jaguar, Buccaneer and – of course – the Vulcan and the Lightning.

An excellent guide to making the best of the best and most enduring British aircraft designs from the post-war era.

## Featuring the work of:

Allen Berry; John Bisset; Mark Chadbourne; Bill Clark; Andy Evans; Jan Forsgren; David Francis; Tony Gloster; Tony Grand; Allan J. Harper; Gary Hatcher; Paul Janicki; Tim Large; Ernie Lee; Andy McCabe; Bernie Montague; Steve Muntus; Keith Peckover; Neil Robinson; Sam Scoles; Ted Taylor and Jack Trent.

# Contents

# Chapter 1

# English Electric Canberra

## English Electric Canberra B(I )8

**TECH PANEL**

| | |
|---|---|
| Scale: 1/72 | |
| Kit No: 05038 | |
| Decal Options: 3 | |
| Panel Lines: Recessed | |
| Status: New Tooling | |
| Type: Injection Moulded Plastic | |
| Parts: Plastic142, Clear 7 | |
| Manufacturer: Airfix | |

By Tim Large

The Canberra more than any other aircraft typifies the success of classic British aircraft design in the aftermath of World War Two. Manufactured in large numbers through the 1950s, the aircraft could fly at a higher altitude than any other contemporary bomber and set a world altitude record of 70,310 ft (21,430 m) in 1957. Due to its ability to evade early interceptors, and its significant performance advancement over contemporary piston-engined bombers, the Canberra was a popular export product and served with many nations.

In addition to being a tactical nuclear strike aircraft, the Canberra served in a variety of roles such as tactical bombing and photographic and electronic reconnaissance. Canberras served in the Vietnam War, the Falklands, the Indo-Pakistani Wars, and numerous African conflicts, and on occasions both of the opposing forces had Canberras in their air forces.

The Canberra was retired by the RAF in June 2006, fifty seven years after its first flight. Airfix have covered a number of variants in both 1/72 and 1/48 with modern injection-moulded kits, which have been ably supported by the aftermarket.

The much anticipated 1/72 B(I )8 arrived, resplendent in an eye-catching red box, decorated with a pair of silver SAAF machines swooping down to deposit their bomb load. Once inside you find a single sealed bag with seven sprues, six of which come in a light grey plastic, holding one hundred and ninety-two cleanly moulded parts. All the panel lines are recessed with the cockpit, bomb bay and undercarriage having the appropriate raised detailing. In its own bag, there is a small clear sprue of seven parts, including the canopy, a clear nose cone, and a side window for the navigator.

A good sized decal sheet, which appears to be well printed, comes with three options, and the build is dealt with by a fourteen-page instructions booklet, which for some reason has the 1/48 B(I) 8's artwork on the cover.

## Construction

The first six sections deal with the cockpit area, which is detailed to an acceptable level, with instrument panels, navigator equipment etc. There is no sidewall detailing, but then again you can't see a whole bunch once the kit is completed. This was then fitted into the fuselage halves, along with the detailed bomb bay and front wheel bay, and the fuselage halves joined together without a hitch, as did the wing and tail assembles. Here the wings have enclosed main wheel bays and nicely moulded inlets and outlets for the engines. One issue I had was the need to use quite a lot of filler to blend in the tailplanes to the rear fuselage, but that was the only such used throughout construction.

The undercarriage, both front and rear, are detailed affairs and more than adequate for a kit of this scale, complementing the wheel bays, and I did like the fact that all the wheels have a flattened bottom. There is a choice of ordnance, consisting of 1,000lb bombs, ventral gun pack, 2" rocket pods and what I presume are Nord AS.30 air-to-surface missiles. Though the B(I) 8 had a nuclear ability, this option is not included in the otherwise comprehensive weapons fit.

Last of all the clear two-part canopy is fitted, along with the wing lights and various aerials, and I also fitted the separate wing flaps at this stage to finish up what had proven to be a pleasurable build.

## Colour Options

If you have Airfix's 1/48th B(I) 8 then you'll be on firm ground, as the options are disappointingly the same. Two aircraft are finished in grey/ green upper surface and light grey undersides and cover 16 Squadron, RAF, Laarbruch West Germany 1972, and 14 Squadron, RNZAF, Ohakea 1968. The third choice is an all-over Silver B(I) 12

from No 12 Squadron, SAAF, Waterkloof 1969 to 1975.

The decals supplied are well printed, in good register, and have a gloss carrier film, though I suspect colour will bleed through the white on the camouflaged aircraft. On the bright side the decals are comprehensive in scope, with full stencilling for all three aircraft, as well as the relevant national and individual markings.

## Conclusions

It's so good to get a major manufacturer giving us a 1/72 Canberra. The last one, in 1975, also from Airfix, was their ill-fated B 2, which was re-tooled into the B-57B and is sadly not in production at the time of writing. The new kit is well moulded, easy to put together, and accurate in dimensions and shape, and all this at a very reasonable price.

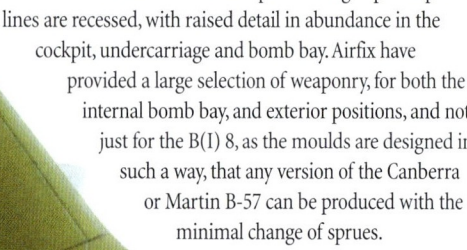

**TECH PANEL**

| | |
|---|---|
| Airfix Canberra B(I) 8 | |
| Scale: 1/48 | |
| Kit No: 10102 | |
| Price: £27.99 | |
| Status: New Tooling | |
| Type: Injection Moulded Plastic | |
| Manufacturer: Airfix | |

# Canberra Test Shot in 1/48

By Tony Gloster

The kit built here was constructed from test shots provided by Airfix prior to the kit's release, so I won't dwell on any minor fit problems or moulding issues as these are to be expected, at this stage of the model's development. Seven sprues of light grey plastic hold 175 parts, with one sprue of clear plastic featuring eight parts. The mouldings were crisp and clean, with no flash anywhere and just a few sink marks on the surface of the four separate wing flaps. All panel lines are recessed, with raised detail in abundance in the cockpit, undercarriage and bomb bay. Airfix have provided a large selection of weaponry, for both the internal bomb bay, and exterior positions, and not just for the B(I) 8, as the moulds are designed in such a way, that any version of the Canberra or Martin B-57 can be produced with the minimal change of sprues.

## Construction

There were no instructions supplied with the kit so I started with the cockpit, which mostly comes on its own sprue and has everything you need. The pilot's area is fully detailed, with raised instruments and switches, as is the navigator's position, including rudder pedals, two types of control stick, and three ejector seats (with seat belts moulded in place). Also included are three crew members, although these seem a bit on the small size. All these parts fitted together well, as did the whole assembly, along with the front wheel bay, when offered up to the fuselage. The fuselage halves were then joined together, needing just a hint of filler on the joint here and there.

The rudder is a separate item of two parts, and fitted perfectly. Before I closed the bomb bay up, weight was added to the useful space above the front wheel bay, as I expected a tail sitter. However, even though I added 117g (that's 4½ oz) when finished it still was not enough, but thoughtfully, Airfix have provided a stand to support the tail.

As I was making the B(I) 8 I did not use the detailed bomb bay, which by the way has a full load of bombs, as the two-part ventral gun-pack was to be fitted over the closed bay doors. The gun-pack had just three gun barrels moulded in place, with one missing? Also the four cannon underside troughs were not present.

The wings come in two main parts, upper and lower, with the ailerons and flaps moulded separately. The flaps, by the way, feature

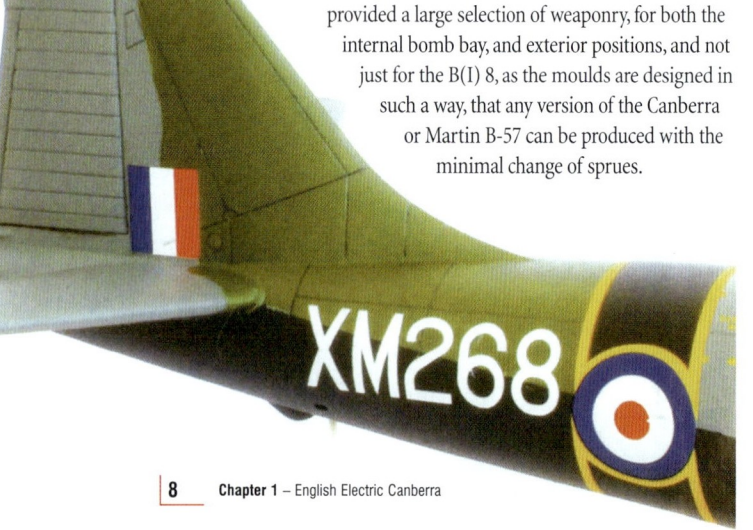

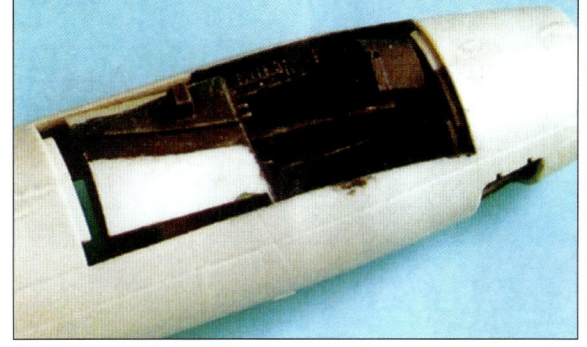

The design of the fuselage allows for different versions of the Canberra to be made, with different canopy inserts

The fighter canopy masked up and ready

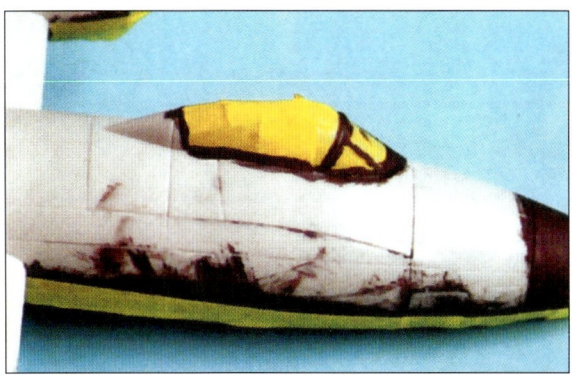

The insert for the B(I).8 is perfect, with no, filler or adjustment being needed

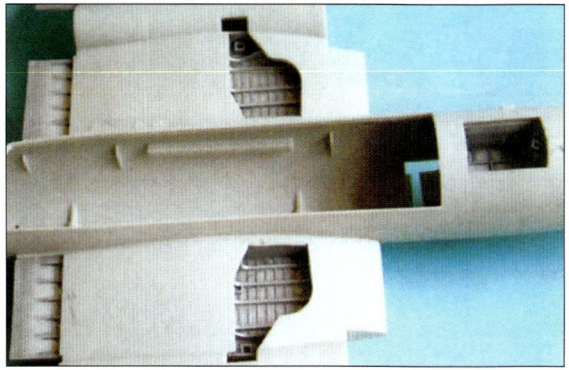

The wheel bays are detailed as are the flaps. The bomb bay was not used in this build, but as you can see the aperture provided is of ample size

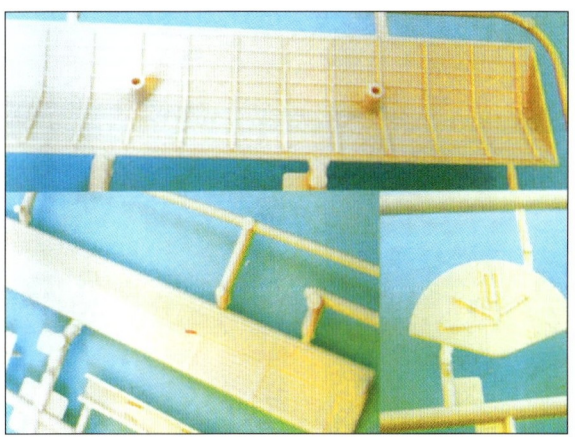

The bomb bay is well detailed

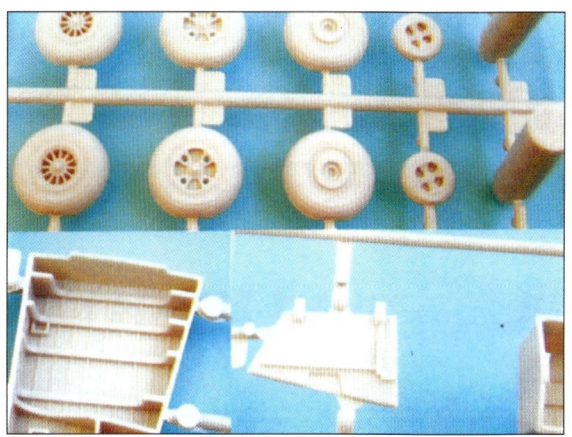

The main wheel bays have ribbing with the doors having detail, note the two types of hub for the wheels

9

full detail on the insides, as do the upper wings. Before the wings are joined together the one-piece mainwheel bays are fitted, and although these are not full depth, they do have the ribbing moulded into them. At this stage you can open up the mounting slots for the underwing hard-points. There are five slots per wing, and I would presume the instructions will guide you as to which is used, depending on which version of the kit you have. In this case I opened out the innermost, as that would seem to be the regular fit of the B(I) 8. There is a choice of weapons for the hard-points, of which I elected to use the multi-rocket pods. The engine intakes and exhausts are separate items, again allowing different version to be offered. The inlets are nicely moulded with good fan detail. The outlets are a one-piece moulding and are full depth with engine detail at the ends. These fit into two-part shrouds, and both inlets and exhaust shrouds fitted with minimal fuss.

I left the major clear parts until last. These consist of a two-part fighter-style canopy and a one-piece nose, which has the two side windows and the clear nose moulded in place. There are no moulding seams on any of the parts (please note, Hasegawa). The flat bomb aimer's panel on the nose is moulded at an angle, and despite conjecture this would appear to be correct, according to my references, though the angle would appear to be a bit extreme. The pilot's canopy is the centre of some very clever designing. In an effort to get as many versions as possible from the same moulds, the section of fuselage above the pilot and engineer is a separate piece, and this enables any type of cockpit configuration to be offered with little fuss. Some concern had been expressed about the potential fit of this part, but on this example it was perfect. I simply put it in place in place and added glue – no filler or rubbing down was required.

The undercarriage was added after the painting was completed. These consist of three one-piece mouldings for the legs, and two separate retraction mechanisms for the main undercarriage, while the front mechanism is moulded with the leg. Two small front wheels are provided with separate mudguards, and the mainwheels come in two parts, with two types of hub. All three assemblies fitted well to the bays. The wheel bay doors have moulded internal detail, though the front ones needed a small amount of modification on the moulded hinges to fit in place.

## Colour Options

I had no dec als with the test shot, so I used the Model Alliance decal sheet MA-48146 *RAF B(I) 8 & PR 9 Canberra's Part 2*. As there are no stencils supplied on the Model Alliance sheet, a quick trip to Hannants, London, produced the 1/48 Xtradecal sheet for the Canberra B 2, which had a set of the needed items, as well as three options for the forthcoming Airfix B 2.

Out of the four B(I) 8 options, (there are five for the PR 9) I selected XM268 from 16 Squadron, based at Bruggen, West Germany 1963. The camouflage finish for this aircraft is black under sides with Dark Sea Grey and Dark Green upper surfaces. All paints used in the build were from the Humbrol range and applied by brush, and once the decals were dry, a final finish of the excellent Mr Hobby Flat coat (H20) was sprayed on.

Overall the Model Alliance decals were of a high quality, and the Xtradecals were trouble free in all departments.

## Conclusion

I can't lavish enough praise on this kit, it's the best fitting Airfix kit I've ever made, and I've made a few over the years! The attention to detail and clever design features make this, in my opinion, possibly the best 'out of the box' Canberra kit made to date and I'm just talking about a test shot. This all bodes well for the future of Airfix in the 21st Century.

**TECH PANEL**

| | |
|---|---|
| Scale: 1/48 | |
| Kit No: 48008C | |
| Type: Resin Conversion Set | |
| Manufacturer: Alley Cat | |
| Available from A2Zee Models | |
| Also used: Airfix #101031 Canberra PR 9 | |

# Accessorise SC 9 Canberra Conversion

## A unique variant based on the Canberra PR 9 in 1/48

By Ted Taylor

This simple but effective conversion kit contains three resin parts, the nose section and two new tip tanks, which have rounder ends on them and seem to be a little fatter. Parts need only a light rub down with your favourite sander after cutting the tanks from the pour blocks, while the block on the nose can be left on as it fits inside the assembled fuselage quite nicely. The decal sheet comes in two parts with roundels and fin flashes on one sheet and serial numbers on the other, while the placement sheet gives information on four different periods of the aircraft's life and the three bases at which it served, namely Pershore in 1970 and 1972, then RAF Wyton in 1976, and finally at RAF St Mawgan in 1985. You get a choice of colour schemes that should keep most modellers happy - overall high speed silver, overall white, raspberry ripple, then hemp and grey.

There are a few faults with the Airfix kit that can be fixed and are noted on various websites. The main one I believe is the angle of the base of the fin, where there is too much of a curve, so I sanded away the leading edge to reduce this. There is just enough thickness of plastic here to do this but wait until the fuselage halves are joined and the cement has cured.

Alley Cat's decal sheet provides four options for the aircraft

The wings have posable flaps and movable ailerons, but I found two extra halves for the ailerons so make sure you use the pairs that make the thinnest part, as the thicker ones will not match the groove they fit into. When the aft ends of the engines are added you may want a little filler, but careful assembly is the secret to get the best fit possible.

The Canberra is a dedicated tail sitter in model form so you will need some nose weights, and the kit advises 100gm but that is nowhere near enough. In the standard PR 9 I used nearly 150gm in the nose cone and it still needed the prop under the tail. In the SC 9 I drilled a short way into the resin nose section and loaded 150 gm of lead shot, and the combined weight was enough to hold it down.

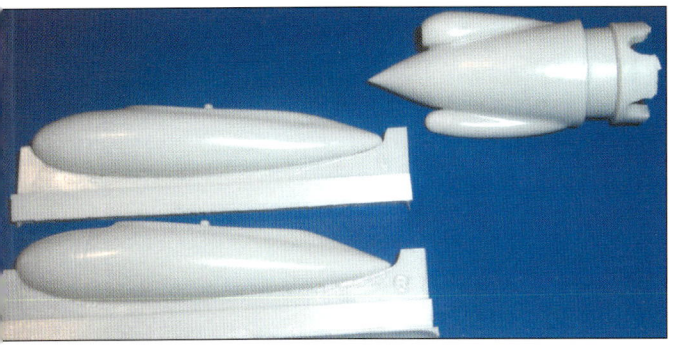

The simple but effective conversion parts

11

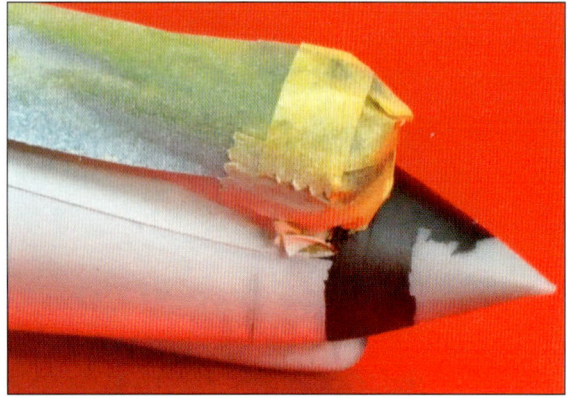

The nose plug in place

New resin wingtip tanks are provided

The standard PR.9 – also from the Airfix kit

The raspberry ripple scheme involves a great deal of masking

Be prepared to expend a lot of Masking tape!

Before you add the camera bay, parts 3H or 4H, there is room above the nose wheel bay that can take a fair amount of weight.

With that kind of weight in the nose there will be a terrific strain on the nose wheel axles so I removed them and replaced them with a short length of brass rod drilled through the leg. I have repeated this on the main wheels on all my Canberras as a precaution. When the tops of the main legs were cemented in position I reinforced the joint with a dab of epoxy resin as the plastic is quite soft.

The raspberry ripple scheme must be one of the most difficult to get right and probably uses more masking tape than any other. I planned for a couple of days how I was going to paint and mask. Firstly I needed a good white base coat to back up the gloss white and the red areas, and for this Humbrol #130 Satin White was sprayed on the entire upper surface and those areas below that needed red. Left for twenty-four hours this was lightly rubbed over with very fine wet and dry before a thin coat of gloss white was sprayed overall. A further twenty-four hours later this was masked off with strips of Tamiya's wide tape ready to receive the red areas, and for this I used Humbrol #19 Gloss Red, as I had no Insignia Red. For the blue I used Revell #53 which matches the Insignia Blue on the decal sheet.

After all the masking was removed and any tiny touch-ups

attended to I masked the edges of the anti-glare panel to spray Humbrol Matt Black #33. The next task was the decal placement and this passed off unevenfully using a combination of kit parts and those provided by Alley Cat. On the PR 9 wing there are vortex generators just where the roundels go and it is very difficult to induce decals to settle down over them even with setting solutions, so I solved the problem by slicing out a strip from the blue area the width of the generators then adding the two parts on either side and painting the generators with a tiny brush using the insignia blue. Various little touches of colour were needed to finish off the painting stage before the remaining parts, such as gear doors and blade aerials, were added. The pitot tubes were cut to length from fine steel hypodermic tube - the type you find on Revell's little Contacta cement dispensers.

I also built the standard PR 9 alongside this model and was amazed when I saw the difference between the two. All-in-all a very satisfying project, well done Airfix/Hornby, and well done Alley Cat.

Alley Cat products are available via A2Zee models, and both the SC 9 conversion, and the Canberra PR 9 are also available in 1/72 from Alley Cat and Airfix respectively.

# Canberra PR .9

## Building a Test Shot of the Airfix 1/48 kit

By David Francis

'How do you fancy building the test shot of Airfix's new Canberra?' Well what would your answer be? Next day a large white box arrived on my doorstep, and on opening it I found two sprues in the familiar grey styrene that you normally associate with modern kits and three in red, blue and lime green, just like a Matchbox kit from the 1970s.

Like most modern products kits are designed on computer, from the individual components to the large metal tools that make them. The first time the kit designers get to see if the kit goes together as planned is when the moulds are run for a test shot. I have heard two versions as to why they are in bright colours, the first is that they just use any plastic left over from other products but the more believable

one is that it is easier to see any moulding problems or flaws on coloured plastics than on grey. One interesting thing on my example was that the red sprue, which included the upper section of the fuselage around the pilot's cockpit, had a number of notes written on it with arrows and crosses indicating that the hole for the antenna post was 30mm too far back, no doubt something that will be changed by the time the kit hits the shelves.

So onto the plastic, and what we have got? The fuselage sprue has the lengthened fuselage of the PR 9 however one small error that is also present on the B(I) 8 still remains and that is the fillet at the front of the fin, which extends too far along the fuselage. Also on this sprue are two alternative bomb bay sections, the first was in use during the 70s and 80s and has five separate camera bays, while the second is more appropriate to a 21st century fit with a large bay at the front for a panoramic camera, and at the rear a massive circular section with a slightly small bay behind it. At the base of each bay there is a representation of a camera lens.

The blue sprue provides the PR 9 wings and these are a lot broader and wider than those fitted to the standard model, and finally the red sprue has all the detail parts, including a selection of antennas and intakes, the cockpit section, a new nose and finally a pair of BOZ107 chaff Flare Pods.

What is missing from the test shot is any form of instructions. As I had nothing to hand on the type I needed to obtain an example of the *Aeroguide* on the Canberra PR 9. This is probably the definitive modellers book on the subject as it has everything you need to really go to town on the Airfix kit, from scale plans to walkaround

**TECH PANEL**

Canberra PR 9

Scale: 1/48

Kit No: 10103

Panel Lines: Recessed

Status: Revised Tooling

Type: Injection Moulded Plastic

Manufacturer: Airfix

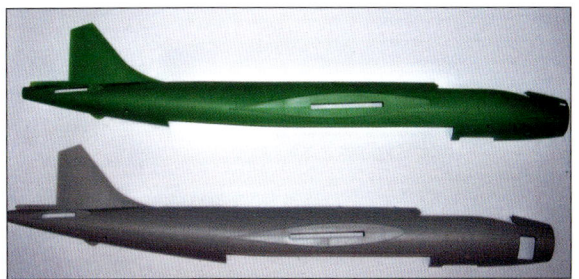

The B(I).8 and PR.9 fuselages compared

Not just empty bays - note the camera lenses at the bottom

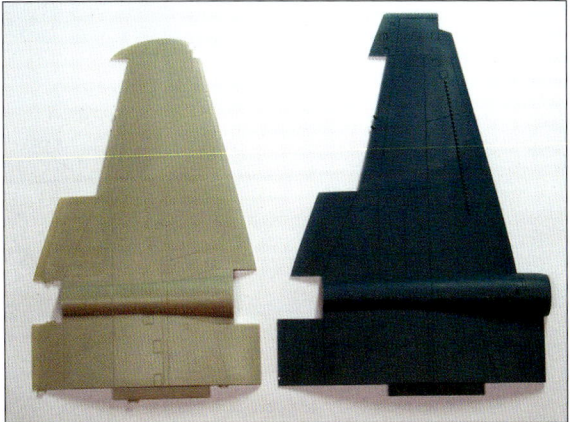

The new wing is bigger in all directions

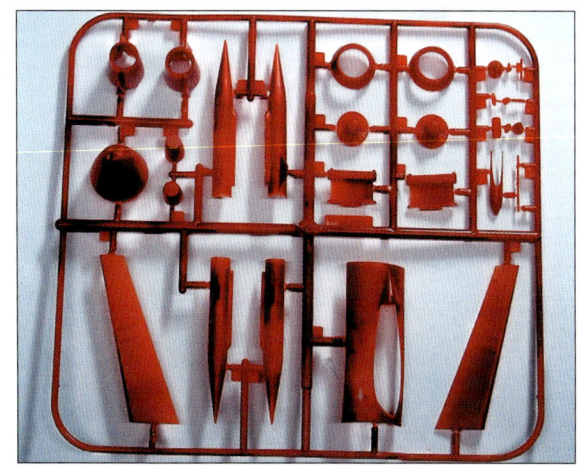

The detail parts - note marks on cockpit sprue

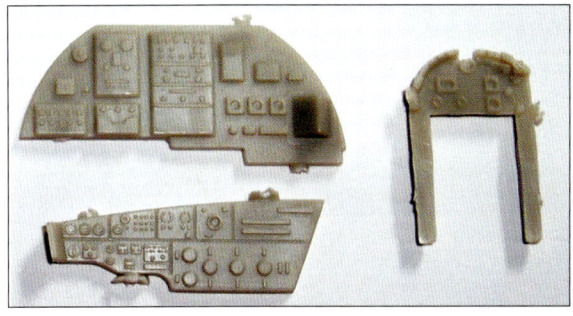

Moulded detail on the parts you cannot see is very good but the instrument panel needs help

My improved cockpit used Mike Grant and MDC instrument decals but is mostly invisible and inaccurate for a PR.9

photographs of all the areas modellers like to work on - like the cockpit, undercarriage bays and camera bays. Of course there are also plenty of photographs covering the forty years of operations and a number of colour profiles; if you are serious about your model I can not recommend this title highly enough.

Using the detail plans in the *Aeroguide* it seems possible to build any PR 9 from 1965 to 2004 with the parts in this kit. In its final years the type was modified to operate in a more hostile environment most noticeably external RWR pods were added to the end of the wings, and these will have to be scratchbuilt if you want to build a post-2005 version unless an enterprising manufacturer produces an update set.

## Construction

As we reviewed the interdictor Canberra previously I am mainly going to concentrate on the specific PR 9 parts, but what I can say from my experience of this kit is that it required the least filler of any I can remember in the last five years, and remember this is a test shot!

The cockpit area is the same as supplied in the earlier kit, which though nicely moulded is inaccurate for any PR 9 - not a problem for me as the interior is primarily black, but for those who want 100% accuracy there is room for some scratch building or the inevitable aftermarket set. As the ejection seat is the most obvious detail I

replaced the kit part with a MB 7 from Aires, which has a higher level of detail plus etched brass seat belts, all for £2.50. Not quite correct for a PR 9 but who's going to know if I keep it quiet.

Once completed the cockpit is located within the separate fuselage upper section. I added a little detail from wire to the rear turtle deck as photographs show two pipes wrapped in red insulation tape in this area, which add a touch of colour to the predominantly black cockpit. The fuselage fit is superb and the bomb bays almost a snap fit.

Bear in mind that this model needs a lot of nose weight, and in the earlier kit they recommended 100gms. I added a 125gm fishing weight and it was still not enough. My mistake I think was to put it behind the cockpit instead of packing the forward nose, but if you do get a tail-sitter Airfix do provide a tail stand just in case.

One thing I included were the small circular camera windows low down on the forward fuselage. One minute with a twist drill and a set of plans and they were added, and after painting filled with Kristal Klear.

Now for my big bug! What is going on with the rudder? This part is common to all Canberras so was moulded in standard grey plastic, but someone had gone overboard with the engraving machine as it is

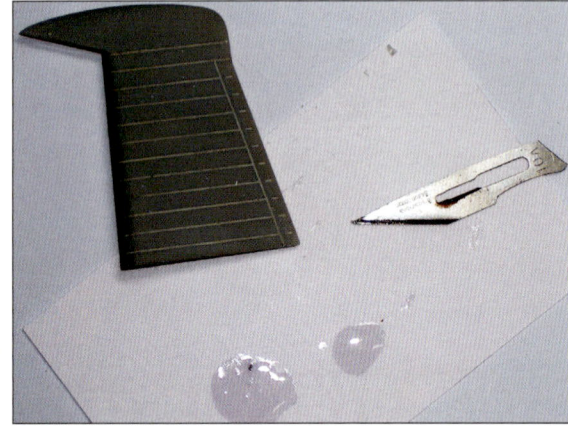

Something needs to be done about that rudder

The panels were livened up with some etched bezels

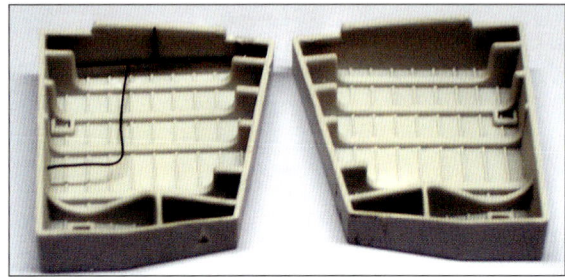

I added a few bits of wire but you can spend a happy hour adding detail to the nice wheel bay

Discs cut from holographic confetti add detail to the cameras

A simple modification is to drill into the rear of the clear parts to produce the bulbs for the navigation lights

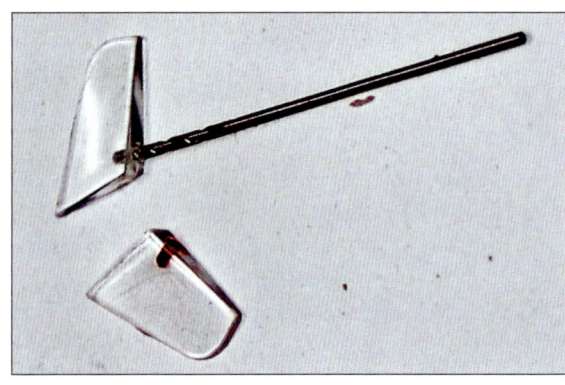

covered with deep horizontal lines. Look at a photograph of a Canberra and you may just make out a few fine dimples but definitely no panel lines. I filled them with typewriter correction fluid and once dry this was sanded smooth, which was about 95% successful but in a few areas the line was still visible so I now fell back on my favourite new trick, using an old scalpel blade to run super glue into the crack and then almost immediately sanding the area with an 800 grit sanding stick to obtain a perfect finish, before attaching it to the tail slightly offset.

I now turned to the wings and engine nacelles, and found these go together easily with just a little bit of sanding needed to ensure all joining areas are flat, and just like the earlier kit you have positionable control surfaces and dropped flaps - which is handy as these are nearly always down when on the ground. The large

navigation lights are supplied on the clear tree and are best fitted after painting but it is best to test fit them now as you will need to sand the wing section back quite a bit to get a perfect fit, and that is easier done before painting is started. At the same time I used a small jeweller's drill to put a hole into the rear surface of the clear part. These holes are then filled with red and dark green paint to represent the light bulbs.

With all the major assembly completed I now added the aerials and intake parts. In some case these are over scale and better replaced with Plasticard. If you look in the *Aeroguide* you will also find that there are a number of small details missing from the kit, most noticeably the two prominent pitot tubes on the port fuselage side just behind the cockpit and the towel rail aerial on the side of the lower fuselage. None of these are hard to reproduce. All other areas of the kit are identical to the earlier version but I must give praise to the wing undercarriage bays which are well detailed out of the box and with a little extra work with wire and rod will look amazing.

## Painting and Decaling

With nearly fifty years of service there are a number of schemes you can choose to paint your PR 9, but for me it had to be one of the Hemp and Grey ones used in the First Gulf War with their mission markings and female nose art.

I used Xtracolour Hemp and Light Aircraft Grey. The glossy surface that Xtracolour dries to is a perfect base for decals and I used Model Alliance sheet ML48146 for the aircraft markings and sheet ML489018 for all the numerous stencils. The only decal you need to be careful with is the two-part nose art, as you get a white base, which is applied first. Once this is dry the second detail decal is added, and this is very thin and needs to be perfectly centred on the white one. I used a pair of tweezers but with hindsight would advise the use of a brush and plenty of wetting agents.

## Conclusion

This kit was a pleasure to build and represents the most aesthetically pleasing of all the British Canberra variants beautifully. The fit of parts is to a high standard and though the engraving may be a bit deep for some tastes, under a coat of paint it will look good.

I was quite happy with the kit out of the box - though on my next two I will add the missing pitot tubes. Another fine new tooling from a revitalized company.

# Chapter 2

**TECH PANEL**

| EE Lightning F 2A/F 6 |
| --- |
| Scale: 1/48 |
| Kit No: 09178 |
| Manufacturer: Airfix |

# English Electric Lightning

## Alpha Mike

### Revisiting Airfix's 1/48 Lightning F 6

By Tony Gloster

There is little that can be said about the incomparable Lightning with its afterburning Rolls-Royce Avon engines and amazing climb-to-height ability. Those who remember this outstanding aircraft in its heyday, when natural metal and flamboyant markings reigned supreme, will have an edge over those of us who recall only their camouflaged era, the grey and green, or latterly air defence grey, but whatever their plumage, the Lightning was a truly classic aircraft, especially if you were fortunate enough to see, hear and feel those Avons lighting-up for take off!

Readers will no doubt have been impressed at the time of its initial release with the Airfix F 6's box art, featuring the prominent shark's mouth that sits so oddly on this particular aircraft. Also evident on the artwork is the name of the pilot, Flt Lt Mike Chatterton.

Although carrying his name, XS903 was not specifically allocated to any single pilot, and all the squadron's aircraft bore the names of aircrew while belonging to a common pool. That the aircraft bears the codes AM – Alpha Mike – may be merely a happy coincidence.

Mike Chatterton joined the RAF in 1975, commencing his flying career on Bulldogs with the Yorkshire UAS. This led on to the Jet Provost T 5 and BAe Hawk, and eventually Mike was selected to train on two-seat Hunters as a prelude to flying Buccaneers — a role as far removed from that of the high-flying Lightning as one could wish.

Following the grounding of the Buccaneer fleet after the Red Flag mishap, and consequent suspension of all training on that type, Mike put himself down for Lightnings, and wound up with 5 Squadron flying the F 6.

As for those sharks' mouths, by all accounts they were applied after

Mixed shades of grey on this trio of 5 Sqn Lightnings (Photo via Mike Chatterton)

The Airfix canopy, with the CMK vacform replacement, above

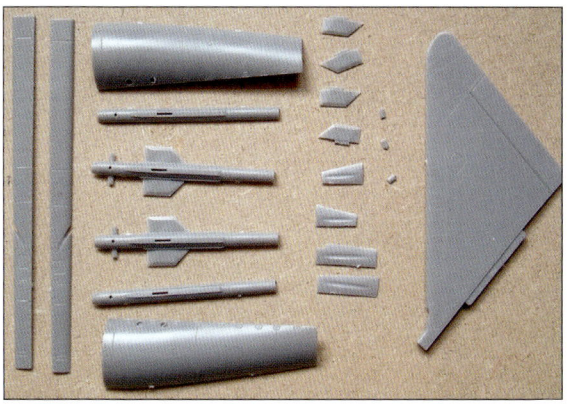

A selection of spare parts!

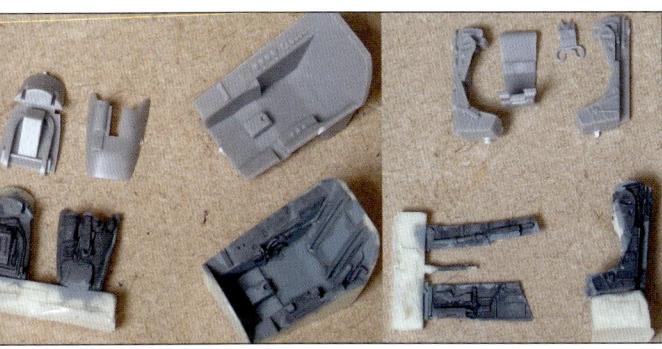

The original Airfix cockpit, with the replacement CMK set, below

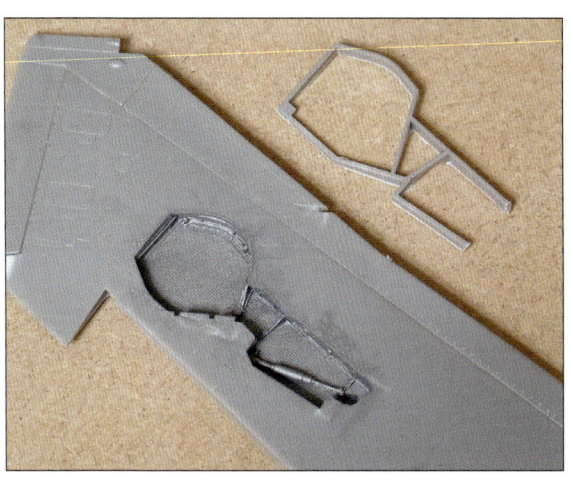

The excellent, despite the fit problems, CMK undercarriage main bays

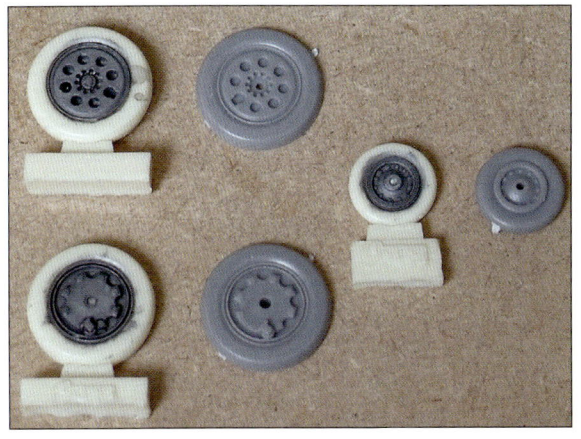

Airfix-supplied wheels are very good, but the resin items are just that little bit better

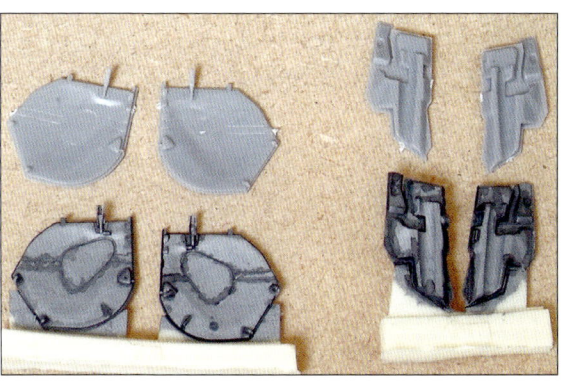

The same can be said for the bay doors

Once I worked out how to fit the thing, the new inlet cone fitted without too much trouble

19

Airfix do make lovely figures

The replacement cockpit

Fitted in and ready to go

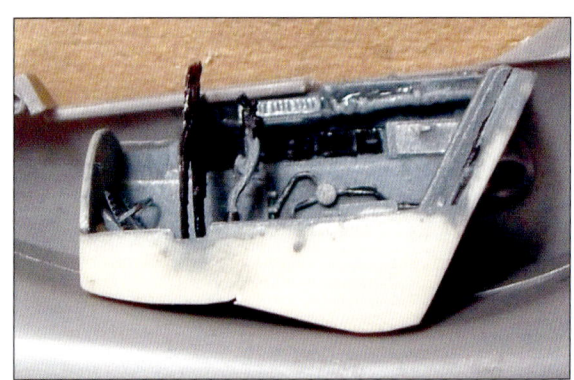

All the internal parts of the kit fitted with no problems

The gun ports were much improved by opening them out, as you can see...

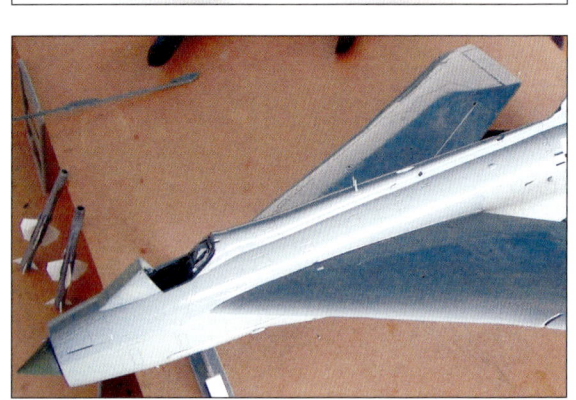

...as was the dorsal air inlet

Painted and drying out

Once painted and fitted the CMK cockpit brings life to the Lightning

the 5 Sqn CO was seconded to an F-106 Delta Dart unit with the USAF. They were not popular with the aircrew on 5 Squadron and were comparatively short-lived.

When Airfix first released their 1/48 Lightnings they were greeted with well-deserved acclaim. A very pleasant surprise awaits inside the large box containing the present kit. You are greeted by five sprues of extremely well moulded light grey plastic. The exterior of the parts is awash with detail, recessed panel lines and sunken rivets, with no flash to be seen. There is one sprue of clear plastic with thirteen parts, a huge well printed decal sheet, and an instruction booklet of twenty five pages, of which eight make up the build; the rest are for the painting and decals of the seven aircraft covered. Some study is needed here as the step-by-step pictorial sections are a bit vague as to where some parts are meant to go. As this kit is the twin of Airfix's F 1-3 it shares many parts on the sprues, with the result that you end up with a whole bunch of surplus bits for the spares box. To this mix, all I added was CMK's cockpit and undercarriage sets, relatively inexpensive, to give the kit that little extra something.

## Construction

What can I say? This was a lovely kit to make, and the overall fit was as good as any kit from the Far East… really. You are supplied with full length inlet and detailed outlets for the engine, a choice of belly gunpack or fuel tank, Firestreak or Red Top missiles depending on the version you wish to make (four in all), refuelling probe and overwing tanks.

The ten-part cockpit as supplied is rather good and with the addition of some etched brass and painting, would look the part, but as I had the CMK replacement, it was put to one side. The new resin parts are finely cast and CMK also give you a small etched sheet in the cockpit set. I found the instructions somewhat confusing however, and far from clear in places. The new cockpit was built up, but without any reference photos of an F 6 cockpit, so I can't vouch for its accuracy.

With some minor adjustments to the tub, sidewalls and cowling, the new cockpit fitted with no headaches and what a difference that made.

Next up I replaced the kit's intake shock cone and front undercarriage bay with the CMK ones, not that there is anything wrong with those supplied by Airfix, apart from the gear bay being a bit sparse. Incidentally, if you do use the kit's parts, Aeroclub make a very clever nose weight.

Did I say the CMK instructions were vague? Well here they made no sense to me (I kid not), and added to this was the fact that the top support on the inlet cone was missing, so I had to use the Airfix part. The rear section was nothing like the drawings, and in the end I worked out what to cut away from the two plastic inlet parts (17 & 18) and how (and where!) to get the cone to fit. Thoughtfully Airfix designed the fit of the parts so the seam line between the two inlet parts is covered by the cone assembly.

The kit's exhaust assembly comes in six parts and with painting come up very nicely indeed. At this stage you have to open out some holes on the two fuselage parts (26 & 27), and add some weight at the front, before fitting together. The fit here again is excellent, but the same cannot be said for the four blanking covers (where the cannon ports go on the F 2A version) as they need some padding out to be flush with the fuselage.

The wings come in five parts each, with boxed-in wheel bays, which were replaced with CMK items, and I had some real problems here, though mostly of my own making. The CMK instructions indicate thinning down of the inside of the top wing parts (#56 & 59) so the new items will fit. I found out it would be a good idea to thin down the underside parts as well as skim a bit off the resin wheel wells themselves, after I glued the wings together! However, due to time constraints, there was not the opportunity to take the wings apart and undertake the necessary surgery.

The cannon ports on the separate, two-part gunpack are not well defined - nor are the ports on the unused separate upper and lower fuselage cannon panels for the F 2A). The gun ports were drilled out, which I am happy to report improved matters.

The kit's undercarriage assembles are nicely moulded, but I still

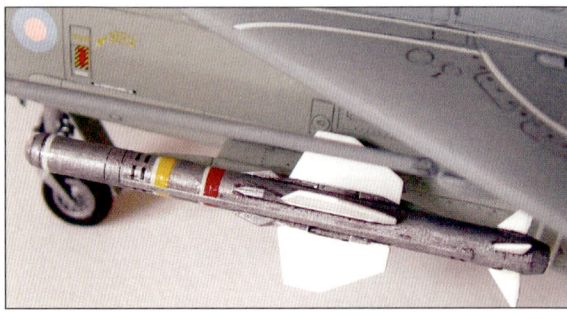

replaced all the wheel bay doors with CMK resin parts, as well as all three wheels. Of the two types of missile that are provided, only the Red Top are used on the F 6. The seven parts that make up each missile 'fell together', the only disappointment being two air bubbles right in the middle of the clear nose lenses (132/3).

The only things missing in the kit are the two azimuth aerials on top of the dorsal spine, which were simply made up from some stretched sprue. Oddly they are shown on the box artwork and the paint and decal guide in the kit's instructions.

## Colour Options

Seven in all, two F 2As both with green upper and natural metal under surface, five F 6s one overall natural metal, one with a grey and green upper and natural metal under surface, two in three-tone grey and one in a two-tone grey finish. As the finish for this build was to be No 5 Squadron's XS903 in the grey three-tone finish, I chose not to use the Humbrol colours, but Hannants Xtracolor, as it has a high gloss finish and takes well to brush work. A trip to Hannants London shop produced RAF Light Aircraft Grey (X15), RAF Barley Grey (X17) and RAF Medium Sea Grey (X3). If there is a drawback to Xtracolor it is that it takes some time to cure. I like to put it the hot sun for a day, which speeds up this process.

Once dry the panel lines were enhanced with Humbrol Matt Grey (27) heavily thinned down and applied with a #1 Winsor & Newton brush.

The decal sheet is generous by anyone's standard, with everything you need. Disappointingly the register is off, the white stencilling is a bit heavy handed, there is a lot of thick carrier film and I felt the low-vis roundels were not the right shade. The roundels were replaced with the Xtradecal sheet X037-48, but

unfortunately, as I could not find any aftermarket decals in print, I had to use the Airfix set.

I used a lot of Micro Sol solution to get them to settle, finding it necessary to soak each one for about half an hour, before being usable, so it took forever to finish it off. Once done and dry the whole model was given a coat of Humbrol matt spray out of the can.

## Conclusion

A really nice kit this one, and you could make a very acceptable model straight from the box, as the quality of the moulding and plastic is first class. The only things that let it down are the one or two badly fitting parts and the poorly printed decals, but I guess you can't have it all. I was not so overjoyed with the CMK resin, finding the instructions difficult to follow, but there are other replacement sets out there and I will take a close look before buying another set when I build the sister kit, the Lightning F 1-3. Saying that, the CMK set's did add to the overall feel of quality surrounding this kit in no small way.

So to sum up, Airfix are on their best form with the Lightning and all with an interest in post-WWII jets should build at least one. Go to the shop now!

Lightning XS903/BA of No.11 Squadron seen in May 1988. The aircraft has the classic black spine and displayed at the 1967 Paris Air Show. Retired in 1987 it now resides at the Yorkshire Air Museum in Elvington

# Bolts from Binbrook

RAF Binbrook near Brookenby, Lincolnshire, served as base for the last two RAF squadrons to employ the English Electric Lightning between 1965 and 1988, and its name is inextricably linked with the type in the hearts and minds of many enthusiasts.

Allan J Harper delves into his photographic archive to look at the latter days of the English Electric Lightning in RAF service.

Lightning F 3 XR718/DE of the Lighting Training Flight taken in April 1986. The aircraft wears a two-tone dark and mid-grey camouflage scheme, with white code letters and serial. First flown in December 1964 this machine went into service with No.56 Squadron. Retired in 1987 at Wattisham, it was transferred to the Blyth Valley Aviation Group in 1992

Lightning F 6 XP693 assigned to British Aerospace as a trials aircraft and seen here in August 1987. Originally on the F 3 production line it was converted to an F 6, spent time at Farnborough and Warton for arrestor hook and gun pack trials, and also served as a Tornado chase aircraft. It was sold to Barry Paver in 1992, and then subsequently sold-on to Mike Beachyhead and shipped to South Africa as part of the 'Thunder City' fleet

Lightning F 3 XP749/DA of the Lightning Training Flight (LTF) taken in October 1984. The aircraft wears the standard RAF grey green camouflage scheme with black serials and white code letters. It first flew in December 1963, was withdrawn from service in 1987 and kept in open storage as 8926M and sold for scrap in January 1988

Lightning F6 XS928 taken in May 1990 when on strength with BAe Systems as a Tornado radar trials aircraft. Withdrawn from use in 1992, the airframe was retained at Warton for display

Lighning F 6 XR726/BE of No.11 Squadron taken in April 1986. The aircraft wears a light two-tone grey scheme with white serials and white codes. First flown in February 1965, it took its final flight in August 1987 and was subsequently sold for scrap in 1992, although the cockpit section was saved

Lightning F 6 XR773/BR of No.11 Squadron taken in October 1987, wearing a two-tone dark and mid-grey camouflage scheme, with white code letters and serial. This aircraft first flew in February 1966 and after serving with No.56 and No.5 Squadrons was placed into storage after its final fight with No.11 Squadron in June 1988. It was eventually sold to Mike Beachyhead in 1997 and shipped to South Africa where it currently serves with the 'Thunder City' fleet

Lightning T 5 XV328 of the Lightning Training Flight taken in August 1987. The aircraft was later broken up and the nose section is now privately owned at Bruntingthorpe

Lightning T 5 XS458/DY of the Lightning Training Flight taken in August 1990, wearing the standard RAF grey green camouflage scheme with black serials and white code letters. First flown in December 1965 it was retired in 1988 and currently remains in a taxiing condition at Cranfield

Lightning F 6 XR724 assigned to the MoD(PE) at Warton and taken in October 1989. The aircraft is seen here wearing a two-tone dark and mid-grey camouflage scheme. Undertook Tornado radar trials and overwing ferry tanks, and sold to the Lightning Association in 1991

Lightning F 6 XS919, in a sorry state, taken in August 1989 while in open storage in Cornwall

Lightning XR770 taken in April 1986 wearing dark grey ferry tanks and IFR probe

**TECH PANEL**

| | |
|---|---|
| Scale: 1/48 | Kit No: 1134 |
| Price: £56.99 US$94.95 | |
| Decal Options: 4 | |
| Panel Lines: Recessed | Status: Reissue |
| Type: Injection Moulded Plastic | |
| Parts: Plastic 109, Clear 10, Resin 4, Etched 114 | |
| Manufacturer: Eduard | |
| UK Importer: Hannants/LSA | |
| US Importer: Squadron | |

# English Electric Lightning F Mk 1A/F 2

## Eduard's limited edition re-issue of the Airfix kit

By Andy McCabe

In 1947 the UK government issued the Ministry of Supply Operational Requirement ER.103 for a transonic research aircraft. English Electric designed and built two prototype aircraft designated as the P 1. The first operational aircraft, a P 1B pre-production variant, arrived at RAF Coltishall in Norfolk in December 1959, and production variants, by then known as the F1, began being delivered from 1960. The improved F 2 Variant first flew on the 11th July 1961 and entered service at the end of the following year.

This Eduard issue is a reboxed version of the Airfix kit with the addition of their own excellent aftermarket products. Having already built two of the Airfix boxings I knew that the kit was a superb one before I began. Two etched sprues and one resin seat, along with express masks and a new decal sheet, are included with the kit, and the etched sprues contain pre-painted parts for the cockpit. There is also a separate glossy colour printed four-sided booklet for painting and applying the four colour options supplied on the decal sheet.

## Construction

The build begins with the cockpit, or more precisely the ejector seat. This is a direct replacement for the plastic part and is a vast improvement as the resin item is superbly cast and detailed. To this are added the seat belts and firing handle from the etched frets.

The cockpit tub has pre-painted etched parts that require the raised parts on the plastic to be removed before they are glued into position, and the instrument panel is a two-part etched construction with the rear part being painted with instrument dials. Etched rudder pedals are also supplied along with throttles, various levers, and cockpit side panels.

Etched parts are also supplied for the front wheel well, which is slightly difficult to fit when the two plastic halves are joined and the location is a bit vague when they are not, so it is a case of 'try it and see' to get the right location. The rest of the intake/forward wheel well is a straightforward plastic assembly.

The next sub-assembly is the exhaust pipes/rear engine faces, and here there are two etched parts that fit into the forward edges of the exhaust pipes before they are joined together.

All of the sub-assemblies are now ready for fitting into the fuselage. No reference is given for nose weight to be added but weight definitely needs to be included. I think that I added approximately 45g of lead strip to the areas above and below the intake, which is really the only place available to put it. The fuselage halves were then joined together.

The next step involves fitting etched main wheel wells, however when these are fitted the underside of the top wing halves will need to be thinned out to allow the wing halves to be joined correctly. The

separate leading edge parts of the wings also took a couple of sessions to align.

The ailerons are separate assemblies that can be portrayed deployed if required, and these are such a tight fit that they could really be left loose if necessary but I felt they were best glued into position.

The model really starts to take shape now as the wings, tail, horizontal tail stabilisers, nose ring, instrument panel coaming and windscreen all go on at the same time, after which the Lightning comes together.

## Colour Options

The windscreen and canopy were masked using a combination of the supplied Eduard Zoom masks and Tamiya masking tape and the canopy was temporarily fixed into position ready for spraying.

The model was now sprayed with a white acrylic primer ready for the main colour scheme to be applied. Four decal options are supplied with the kit, which are:-

● Lightning F Mk 1A, XM184/A, No111 Squadron 1962, natural aluminium with a black dorsal spine and tail
● Lightning F Mk 1A, XM172/B, No56 Squadron, 1963, Firebirds Aerobatic Display Team. Natural aluminium with a red dorsal spine and tail and leading edges to wings and tailplanes
● Lightning F Mk 2, XN786/D, No92 Squadron, Gütersloh, Natural aluminium with a blue dorsal spine and tail

● Lightning F Mk 2, XN794/WW, No19 Squadron Gütersloh. Natural aluminium under surfaces with dark green upper surfaces

Having opted for the Firebirds aircraft Tamiya X-7 Red was sprayed to all appropriate areas and allowed to dry before being masked ready for the next stage. Tamiya X-1 Gloss Black was now sprayed on all over before the application of a coat of Alclad Polished Aluminium.

Once dry and the masking removed the decals were applied and a coat of Johnson's Klear added to seal the paintwork, along with a dark wash to reveal the panel and rivet lines. I then decided to apply a coat of clear acrylic lacquer, which turned out to be a big mistake as it reacted with the Alclad and virtually removed it. Luckily I had been cautious spraying the lacquer on and stopped as soon as I realised, so the damage was not too bad. A valuable lesson was learned, as I should have applied another coat of Johnson's Klear instead.

The model was now put to one side so that I could get on with the undercarriage. These are the standard Airfix parts but have Eduard etched details to go on them. Once assembled and painted they were fitted to the model along with the undercarriage doors and any parts left off during painting. The missiles were also assembled and painted, but as I was modelling a display aircraft I was uncertain as to whether these aircraft carried weapons, but a quick search on the Internet revealed images of Firebirds' aircraft armed.

## Conclusion

The basic Airfix kit is an excellent tooling to which Eduard have added their equally excellent resin and etched products. The cockpit is turned into a really superb replica, and there is a myriad of other etched parts included that really enhance the basic kit and turn it into an outstanding model of the Lightning. The decals are excellent and did not require any setting solutions, which is probably just as well as they also affect the Alclad.

This was a really enjoyable project. I like kits like this that incorporate multi-media parts such as Eduard's pre-painted etch and their new finely cast resin seats. This will prove to be a popular kit, no doubt, as the Lightning was and still is a favourite of many aircraft modellers - this one included. I loved every minute of the build, and I hope the photos do it justice.

27

# Chapter 3

# Gloster Meteor

## Pioneer Propjet

**Modelling the turboprop Gloster Trent Meteor from Unicraft's conversion set and Airfix's Meteor F 1**

By Tony Gloster

The Gloster Meteor was the first British jet fighter commencing operations in July 1944. Thousands were built to serve in the RAF and other air forces, and remained in use for several decades. The Meteor saw limited action in the Second World War, while aircraft of the Royal Australian Air Force served in Korea, and other operators such as Argentina, Egypt and Israel also flew Meteors in regional conflicts. As of 2011, two Meteors, WL419 and WA638, remained in active service with the Martin-Baker company as

ejection seat test beds.

On 7 March 1945 Gloster Meteor F 1 EE227 was sent to the Rolls-Royce plant at Hucknall for installation of two RB.50 Trent turboprop engines. EE227 was selected because it was already fitted with an enlarged wing spar so the new engines could be installed without much further modification. The Trent engine was a Rolls-Royce Derwent II turbojet fitted with a flexible 'quill' drive shaft, a reduction gearbox and a 95-inch diameter five-bladed Rotol propeller.

On 20 September the Trent Meteor took to the air for the first time at Church Broughton airfield with Gloster's chief test pilot Eric Greenwood at the controls, making the world's first flight of a turboprop-powered aircraft. Its career almost ended there and then, for on landing, Greenwood throttled right back and the propeller blades went into the zero-pitch position used for starting. The Trent Meteor effectively fell out of the sky, but Greenwood rapidly applied power and saved the day.

A number of problems had been found with propwash and directional instability, and the Trent Meteor was returned to Hucknall for 'fixes' to be devised. It was flying again by March 1946. Later, smaller 58-inch diameter Rotol propellers were fitted, and the diameter of jet pipes was reduced. In April 1948 the aircraft was transferred to the Royal Navy for testing suitability of turboprop aircraft for deck-operations. It went back to Rolls-Royce on 22 September of that year and was restored to its original configuration before being returned to RAE Farnborough. It was scrapped in June

| GENERAL CHARACTERISTICS | |
|---|---|
| Crew: 1 | |
| Length: 44 ft 7 in (13.59 m) | |
| Wingspan: 37 ft 2 in (11.32 m) | |
| Height: 13 ft 0 in (3.96 m) | |
| Powerplant: 2 × Rolls-Royce Derwent 8 turbojets, 3,500 lbf (15.6 kN) each | |
| Maximum speed: 600 mph (522 knots, 965 km/h, Mach 0.82) at 10,000 ft (3,050 m) | |
| Range: 600 mi (522 nmi, 965 km) | |
| Service ceiling: 43,000 ft (13,100 m) | |
| Rate of climb: 7,000 ft/min (35.6 m/s) | |
| **ARMAMENT** | |
| Guns: 4 × 20 mm British Hispano cannon | |
| Rockets: Provision for up to sixteen "60lb" 3 in rockets under outer wings | |

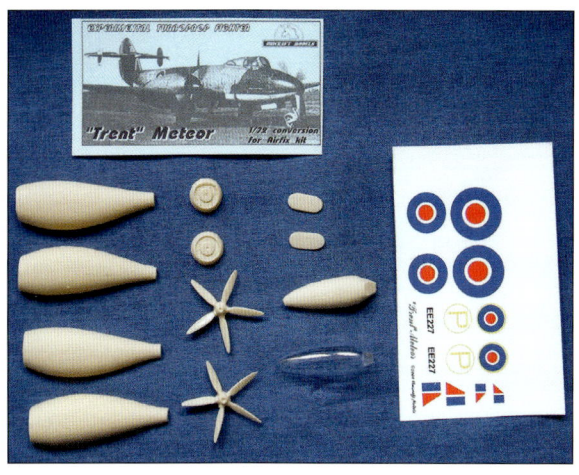

The conversion comprises twelve resin parts, a vacform canopy, a set of decals, a three-view layout plan and a short but interesting history

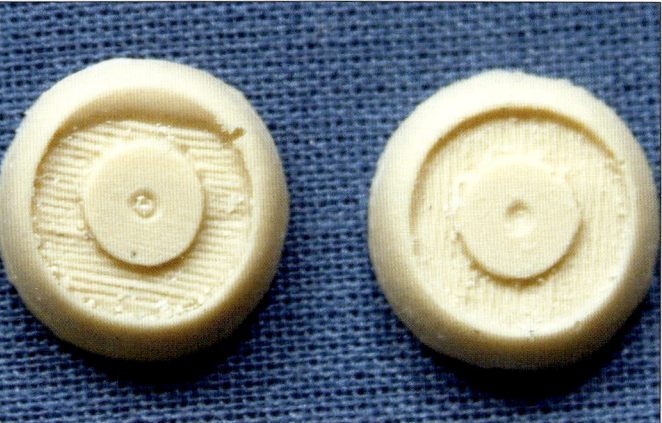

A littler filling makes short work of the air bubbles

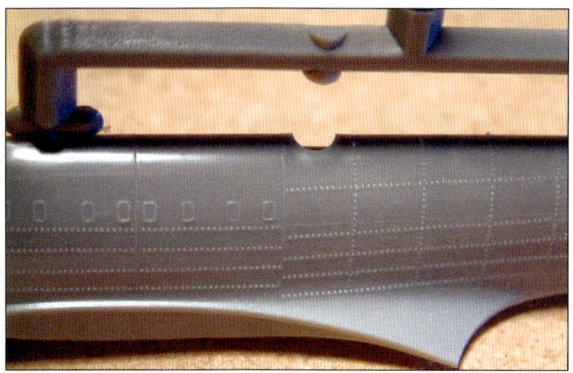

Typical early-Airfix riveting and raised panel lines

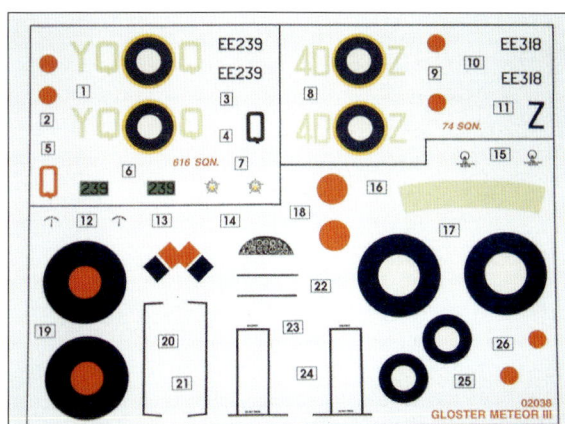

The boxing used for this conversion was a latterday one, with an updated and much improved decal sheet

The resin features air bubbles on all inner surfaces, but these do not present any problems in the build

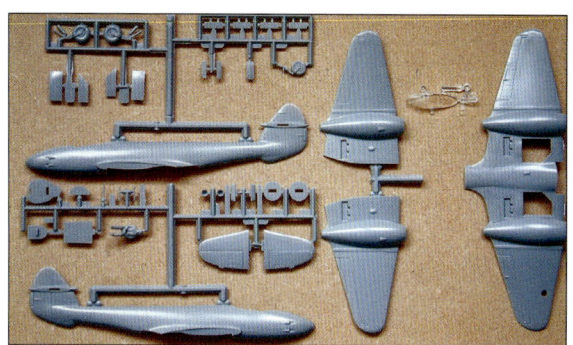

Airfix's Meteor was first kitted in 1969

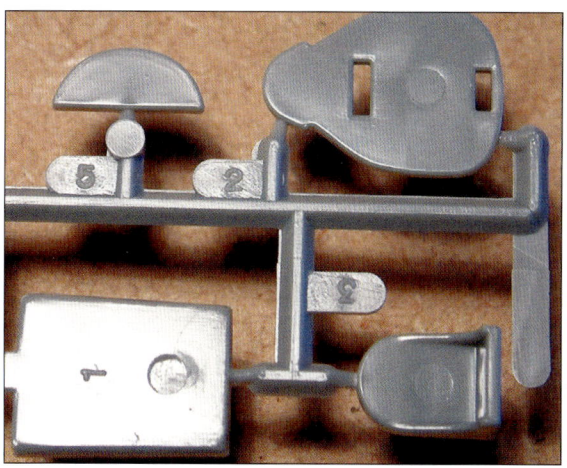

Although simple by today's standards, the kit interior was comprehensive for its day...

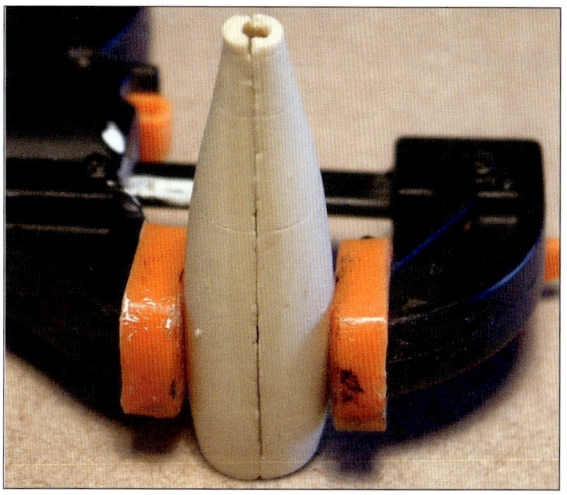

The Trent engines needed a little filling around the pods

Cleaning up the resin props

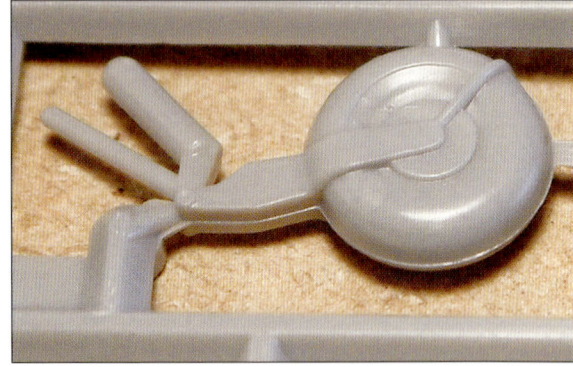

The kit's undercarriage was replaced

The Airfix nosewheel was replaced with that from Matchbox's Meteor NF 11/13

The vacform canopy supplied will require some adjustment to the fuselage to fit

The gun ports were filled in with Squadron White Putty

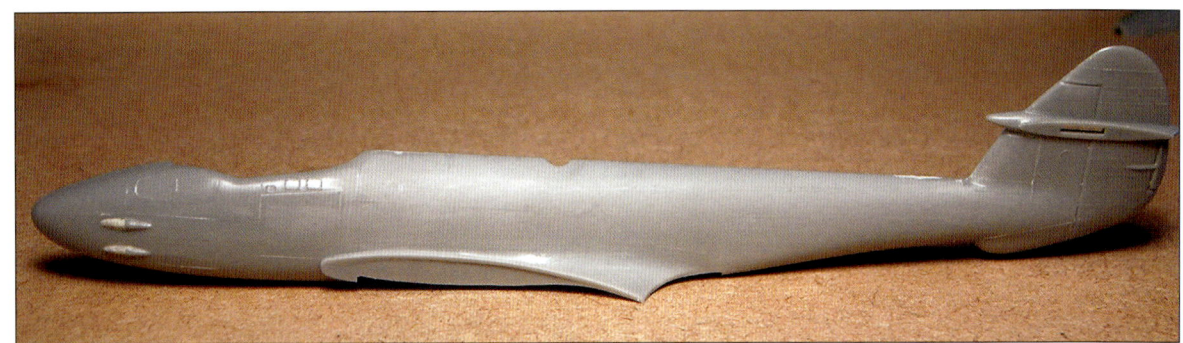

A firm fit was achieved in the end

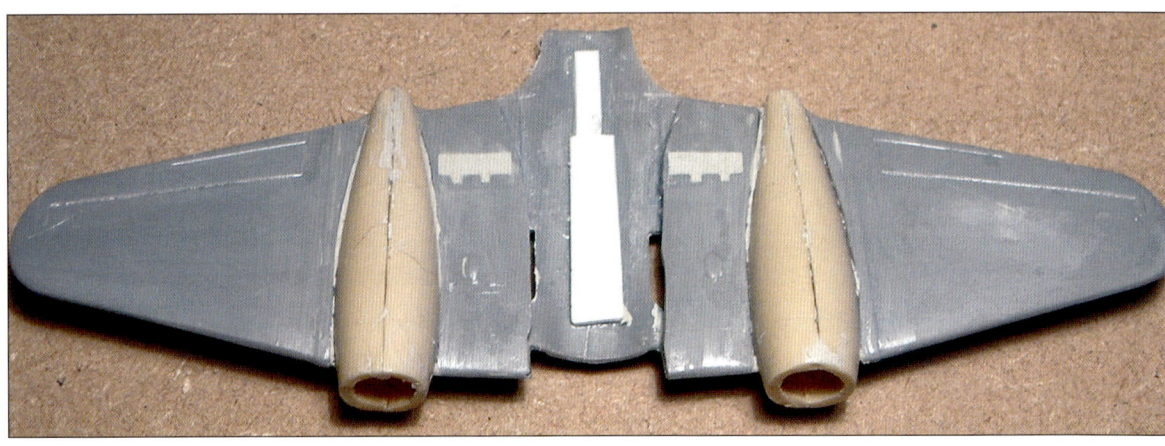

Some rudimentary work was done to improve the interior

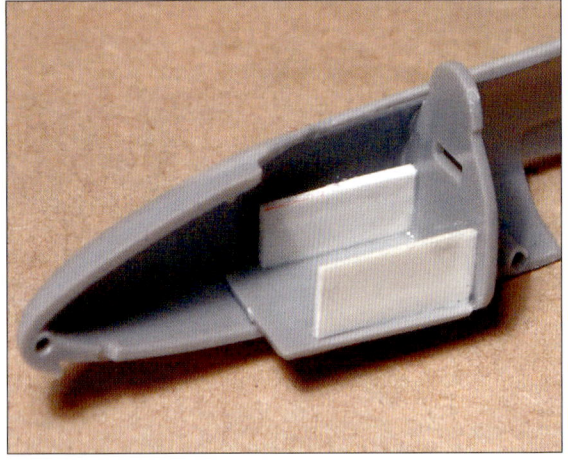

The control column was made from stretched sprue

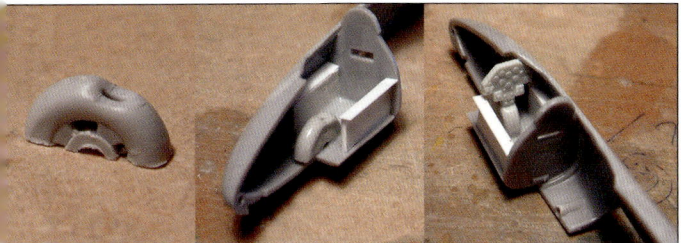

The instrument panel also came from the Matchbox NF 11/13

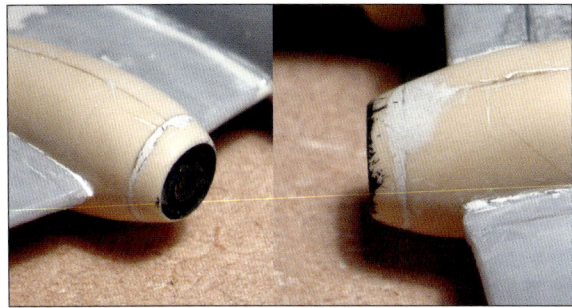

Gaps were filled to contour the lip on the underside of the engine/intake

Positions of the four auxiliary fins were marked out with reference to the plans supplied by Unicraft

The headrest was reshaped to represent that of the earlier variant

1949 with just forty seven flying hours logged. Nonetheless, data gathered by the aircraft proved invaluable in development of Rolls-Royce's later turboprops, notably the legendary Dart.

## The Unicraft Conversion

This little gem arrived from Unicraft's home in the Ukraine in a stout cardboard box tied with string! Inside, a polybag housed the kit, which consists of twelve sand-yellow coloured resin parts, a vacform canopy, a set of decals, a three-view layout plan and a short but interesting history.

A little slip supplied with the kit informs you that 'The model parts are made of brittle resin.' No kidding? It does not travel well regardless of the packaging, and in this case the propeller blades were broken. The resin is home to a large population of air bubbles on all inner surfaces, but these do not present any problems in the build, and the odd one or two on the outer surfaces are easily seen off with filler.

The good thing about the resin used it that it is very easy to carve and sand in the clean-up process, which is just as well as some of the castings do need TLC to get them up to a usable standard. Once this has been done you can turn your attention to the donor kit.

## Airfix's Meteor

First made in 1969, the venerable Airfix Gloster Meteor Mk III is still the only 1/72 scale kit available of the early Meteor. It is made up of 37 parts with raised panel lines and rivets, and has a cockpit interior that looks rudimentary now but was something to shout about back then! This was state-of-the-art when released.

## Conversion

After the various parts had been cleaned up, work began. The first thing to be done was to build up the Trent engine pods. These needed some help when gluing together and there was a bit of filling to do around the joints. This is not unusual with a Unicraft model and part of the joy of making one. Do not fit the front air intake at this stage. If you do, when you go to fit the pods to the wings you will find that the intakes will be facing upwards at a unrealistic angle and will have to be prised off again. Take it from me, I know! Once the pods were dry I put them to one side and started work on the propellers. There was not a lot to do here, just a matter of repairing the damage caused in transit, then cleaning them up and filling in the air bubbles. Work then began on the donor kit. Just how far you want to go here in

preparation (read where to stop) is up to you. In my case the first step was to replace the undercarriage, as the kit's is a little 'flat'. Luckily I had a spare set from a FROG/Novo Meteor IV, but the mainwheels were misshapen and were replaced with items from a Heller Messerschmitt Me 262. The Airfix nosewheel was replaced with that from Matchbox's excellent Meteor NF 11/13. Rivets were rubbed down with some 600-grit wet 'n' dry paper. The only rescribing I did was to redefine the control surfaces. The gun ports were filled in with Squadron White Putty. At this stage I dry-fitted the vacform canopy as the fuselage around the cockpit area needs to be adjusted to suit. As an alternative Unicraft supply a solid resin canopy which does away with the need for any work to the cockpit interior.

Work on the wings consisted of cutting out the engine nacelles and gluing upper and lower wing parts together. The replacement Trent engines needed much dry-fitting to ensure a strong bond as the nacelles are different to those of the F 1's original R-R W2B Welland engines, being somewhat flatter. With the aid of Zap CA glue a firm fit was achieved in the end. Next day the gaps were filled with putty and drops of CA applied to reinforce the joints. At the same time the engraved airbrakes were filled and raised panel lines removed.

I had already prepared the fuselage exterior, so work here was now concentrated on the cockpit. Airfix supply the floor, seat and rear bulkhead, and I as was not 'going to town' on this kit it was just a matter of building up the sidewalls with plasticard. The nosewheel well was made from a half of a Novo Meteor Mk IV mainwheel, which just needed its hub filling with putty — note the convenient air hole on which to rest the instrument panel, which came from the Matchbox NF 11/13. The control column was made from stretched sprue. And that was about it, apart from painting with Humbrol matt black, dry-brushing with silver and picking-out the instruments with

31

Humbrol clear poly. The Sutton-type seat harness was made out of masking tape. Once the two fuselage halves had been glued together the space behind the pilot's seat was covered with a piece of plasticard cut to size then fitted from below, then finished off with filler. Positions of the four auxiliary fins were marked out with reference to the plans supplied by Unicraft, and the fins fitted.

It was now time to return to the engine pods. Once the angle of the intakes had been adjusted to my satisfaction I glued them in place, filling gaps with more filler to contour the lip on the underside of the engine/intake. Next came the canopy, which was not too much of a problem because of the preparatory work done at the start of the conversion, but first I had to fill the gap at the front of the cockpit where the Airfix Mk III's canopy extended further forward than that of the Mk I. I also reshaped the headrest to represent that of the earlier variant. The canopy itself was trimmed to shape and glued into place with Kristal Klear. It looked a touch big to me, especially when compared to the Tamiya 1/48 Meteor Mk I, but it was all there was with the kit and I doubted that many would notice.

## Painting and Decaling

For most of its life EE227 had an unkempt appearance, as it was used as a testbed for a number of projects involving several bouts of modification. In one form it had a cut-down fin, hence the fin flash below the tailplane. After it had been used for some time as the Trent testbed (with the full-height fin/rudder restored), it appears to have been repainted with a high gloss finish, but retained the lower fin flash. This later version of the aircraft was the one I chose to represent.

Hannants Xtracolor was used, RAF Dark Green (X1) and RAF Dark Sea Grey (X4) camouflage above with RAF Trainer Yellow (X11) below. As is my wont the paint was applied by brush and the model put to one side for around a week to dry fully. At this stage the control surfaces were picked out in matt black, and after the decals had been applied the whole model was coated with Humbrol clear poly to give a gloss finish.

Decals came from the Airfix kit, as Unicraft's did not look up to the job, being the wrong shade as well as the printing not being the best I've seen. Neither were Airfix's the best ever made, with the colours not being 100% correct and the white a little transparent, letting the surface colour bleed through, but they did settle down very well with

The canopy was trimmed to shape and glued into place with Kristal Klear

the use of Micro Set and Sol. The prototype 'Ps' were from Joe's Decals sheet # 7201 *WWII Secret and Experimental Aircraft*.

## Conclusion

An unusual model, and chances are that no-one else will have one as I think this is the only conversion kit of this history-making aircraft. Come to think of it, the Airfix donor kit is the only 1/72 kit of an early Meteor. Even though the Unicraft conversion set was not the best example of resin casting I'd ever seen, needing a lot of work, time and patience, in the end it was worth it. What's more, if you have never made a Unicraft kit it's a good starting point and will introduce you to their weird and wonderful world of unusual subjects.

## References

● *Modellers Datafile: The Gloster & AW Meteor*, by R J Caruana and R A Franks. SAM Publications, ISBN 0-9533465-8-7
● *Gloster Meteor*, by Barry Jones. The Crowood Press, ISBN 1-86126-162-4

The paint was allowed a week to cure properly

# Great Balls of Fire

## Meteor Strikes

By Jack Trent

Given its position in the scheme of things – as Britain's first operational jet – it is hardly surprising that the aircraft's story is a emotive one, with a great many variants, and widespread use by different services. Even within the narrower sphere of RAF operations the Meteor's record needs some clarification, and entering mainstream service as the Cold War gathered pace – a period of almost frantic research and development for military technology in all branches – it is hardly surprising to find an almost profligate approach to the type's development.

Gloster received the order for prototype development in February 1941, following Whittle's early successes with jet-powered fighters, and by June of that year a requirement was placed for 300 aircraft, to be named 'Thunderbolt', although this was changed to 'Meteor' to avoid confusion with the P-47. The aircraft was of all-metal construction with a tricycle undercarriage and conventional low, straight wings, featuring turbojets mid-mounted in the wings with a high-mounted tailplane to keep it clear of the jet exhaust.

Delays with the engines meant that it was not until March 1943 that the first aircraft took flight – the fifth prototype, DG206, powered by two de Havilland Halford H.1 engines – and by January 1944 the majority of design problems had been overcome and a production design approved. The first Meteor F.1, EE210, carried four nose-mounted 20 mm (.79 in) Hispano Mk V cannons and the engine was switched to the Whittle W.2, by then taken over by Rolls-Royce. The first twenty aircraft were delivered to the Royal Air Force on 1 June 1944, and one was also sent to the US in exchange for a Bell YP-59A Airacomet for comparative evaluation.

After a conversion course at Farnborough for the six leading pilots, the first aircraft was delivered to 616 Squadron at RAF Culmhead on 12 July 1944. The squadron moved to RAF Manston and, within a week, thirty pilots were converted. The jet had arrived.

The RAF's first jet combat missions saw the Meteor in action against the V1 flying bomb, with interceptions taking place over Kent from 27th July 1944, although after the V1 threat had been superceded by the V2 the type was not allowed to operate over German-held territory, so 616 Squadron briefly moved to RAF Debden to allow USAAF bomber crews to gain experience in facing jet-engined interceptors. Thereafter moving to Colerne, the squadron gained its first F 3s in December 1944, then moved to Europe, where it flew armed reconnaissance and ground attack operations. By the war's end the Meteor was credited with forty-six German aircraft destroyed, although none of them in air combat.

The F 4 followed in 1946, with export orders as well as RAF machines seeing production accelerate, while the F 8, the definitive production model, followed in 1949, by which time the type was in widespread use with RAF frontline squadrons. The T 7, a modified two-seater for jet-conversion and advanced training, was also tested in 1949 and was accepted by the RAF and the Fleet Air Arm and became a common addition to the various export packages, with over 650 manufactured.

The F.8 entered squadron service in late 1950, with widespread exports to various European countries, as well as to Australia and the Middle East where the type was employed by both Israel and Egypt in the Suez Crisis in 1956. Australian Meteors served in Korea, where the shortcomings of the design, in an age of fast swept-wing fighters, was highlighted.

The nightfighter was based on the T 7 twin-seater, using the fuselage and tail of the F.8, and the longer wings of the F 3, while an extended nose contained the AI Mk 10 Air Intercept radar. As a consequence the 20mm cannon were moved into the wings, outboard of the engines.

By the time the final night fighter variant was introduced in 1954, the Meteor was long past its best, and these NF 14s lasted barely into

Meteor F 3s from 56 Squadron on a sortie from RAF Bentwaters, July 1946

1956 before being replaced by the Gloster Javelin. As a front line fighter the type was obsolete, and, like the Royal Navy's Supermarine Attacker, had never really found its place among the accelerated weapons technologies of the dangerous postwar world.

In summary, despite almost global use, the Meteor never demonstrated an ability to hold its own in combat. The RAAF's experiences against the MiG-15, while speaking volumes for the courage of its pilots, clearly demonstrated the type's limitations. Designed in the 1940s, it had no real business offering itself as a front line contender in the 1950s, and one can only wonder what might have come to pass had the Cold War turned hot while so many of the type were still operating with RAF Germany.

From the mid-fifties onwards the Meteor dwindled in service through the familiar route of second-line units – trainers, target tugs, drones, and ground-instruction frames – and while the aircraft holds a significant place in the affections of those fans of classic British aviation, history suggests that these were the roles in which it excelled.

## VARIANTS

Meteor F 1

Meteor F 2

Alternative engined version – only one built

Meteor F 3

Derwent I powered with sliding canopy. 210 built

Meteor F 4

Derwent 5-powered with strengthened fuselage, 489 built by Glosters and 46 by Armstrong Whitworth for the Royal Air Force

Meteor FR 5

One-off fighter reconnaissance version of the F 4

Meteor T 7

Two-seat trainer variant of the F 4

Meteor F .8

Longer fuselage, greater fuel capacity, standard ejection seat and modified tail

Meteor PR 10

Photo reconnaissance version of the F 8. 59 built for the RAF

Meteor NF 11

Night Fighter variant. 311 production aircraft for the RAF

Meteor NF 12

Longer nosed version of the NF 11 with American AN/APS-21 radar

Meteor NF 13

Tropicalised version of the NF 11

Meteor NF 14

NF.11 with new two-piece blown canopy

Meteor U 15

Target drone conversion of the F 4, 92 modified by Flight Refuelling

Meteor U.16

Target drone conversion of the F 8, 108 modified by Flight Refuelling

Meteor TT 20

High speed target towing conversion of the NF 11 for the Royal Navy

Meteor U 21

Target drone conversion of the F 8 for the Royal Australian Air Force by Flight Refuelling

33

# Meteor Shower

## Xtrakit's Gloster Meteor T Mk 7

By Sam Scoles and Allen Berry

The Gloster Meteor T Mk 7 was a two seat trainer based on the Meteor F Mk 4 but with a longer nose to make room for the two man cockpit. It was discovered later that the longer nose actually improved the directional stability of the aircraft. The first aircraft was rebuilt from a machine that was damaged during a sales tour of Europe when the main undercarriage members collapsed during a landing at Melsbroek by a Belgian pilot who lacked experienced on jet aircraft. The impetus was provided by Argentina who had ordered 100 Meteor F Mk 4s with pilot training included in the contract. Gloster found that it would be much safer if the instructor was in the aircraft with the trainee pilot and so the T Mk 7 was born.

### The Kit

The kit comes in a very sturdy top-opening box containing two sprues of light grey plastic and one sprue of clear. As with most limited-run kits, the plastic is thick in places and the sprue gates can

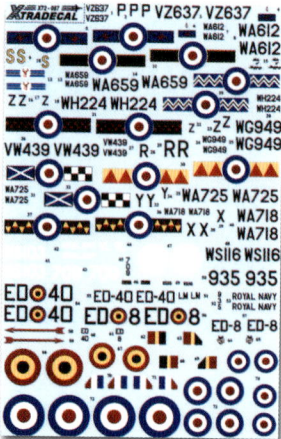

be quite large, so extra care needs to be taken when removing parts. Also in the box is a small decal sheet printed by Aviprint, a sheet of vinyl masks for the canopy and a ten page A5 instruction booklet, which includes a brief history, a sprue layout and painting guide.

### Construction

As I now had three to do I drafted my partner in to help me so they could all be built at the same time. Construction starts with the cockpits. All the side walls, instruments and seat were assembled and then sprayed Tamiya Nato Black (XF-69), and once dry the instrument faces were picked out with an off white and the entire assemblies had a black oil wash. The cockpits were mounted into the port fuselage half and we crammed as much weight as we could into the noses at this point.

Steps nine and ten are for constructing the tailplanes and the fuselage halves. Care should be taken here as, although there are locating tabs on both fuselage halves for the cockpit tub one of ours didn't line up correctly, which resulted in a small gap on the top of the

### TECH PANEL

| | |
|---|---|
| Gloster Meteor T Mk 7 | |
| Scale: 1/72 | |
| Kit No: 72005 | |
| Type: Injection Moulded Plastic | |
| Manufacturer: Xtrakit | |
| UK Importer: Hannants | |
| US Importer: Squadron | |

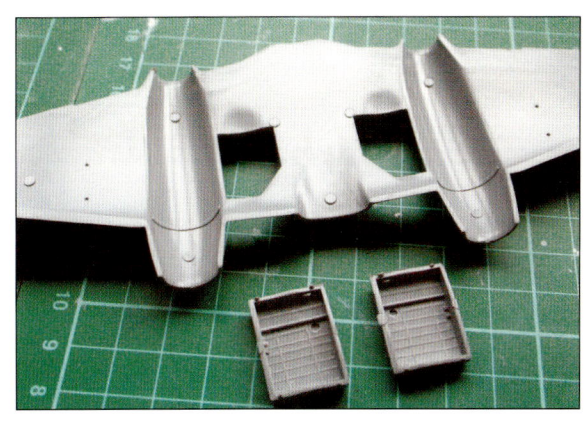

spine behind the cockpit and on the nose in front.

The next few steps are for the wings, engine faces and the exhausts, which are well detailed despite not being very visible once they are mounted in the nacelles. Unfortunately there are a few injector pin marks in the intake walls, the exhausts, and overlapping where the main wheel bays mount to the bottom half of the wing, so out came the trusty micro chisel and sandpaper.

The intake trunks and engine faces were painted matt black with the detail on the faces picked out with a dry brush of aluminium, the wheel bays were glued into place and the wing halves mated – don't forget to drill the holes for the drop tanks if you are mounting them). Wings, tailplanes, intake rings and exhausts were attached and finally we added the one-piece canopies and the models were ready for painting.

### Painting and Decaling

The first job was to mask the canopies, and normally we would get the Tamiya tape out but due to the size of some of the glazing we opted to give the pre-cut vinyl masks a go. The masks are beautifully cut but a little bit on the thick side, and as such there was some difficulty getting the masks for the tops of the canopies to conform to the curved shape. Once the masks were on, the models were primed with grey primer, checked for any flaws, and corrected as necessary. Then the models were ready for painting. We decided to opt for a wide variety of schemes, so I opted to do WA659 of 33

Sqn, from the Xtradecal sheet, while Allen did WL380 of 74 Sqn, from the kit, and WS103/709 of Station Flight RNAS Yeovilton, also from the Xtradecal sheet.

### WA659 of 33 Sqn RAF Middleton St. George circa late 1950s

The Aluminium needed to be painted first, and this was duly applied using Alclad II Aluminium. Once dry I masked off all the areas that were to remain in the natural metal finish and sprayed a light coat of Halfords white primer decanted through the airbrush. This was followed by airbrushing the red onto the nose, the band around the fuselage and tail area and the red parts of the wing tips. The instructions call for Dayglo Red but as I could not find this colour I opted to use Xtracrylix Red Arrows Red (XA1014). Once dry I masked all the red areas and followed up painting the underside with Xtracrylix RAF Trainer Yellow (XA1011). Then came the difficult part of masking the yellow for the black stripes, but after several hours of applying and removing tape I was finally happy and the stripes were sprayed on. All the masking tape was removed and a coat of Klear was applied. The Xtradecal sheet is in excellent register and settled down nicely after an application of Micro Set and Micro Sol. You do only get the bare essential marking with this decal sheet so the stencils were used from the kit decals.

### WL380 of 74 Sqn RAF Horsham St Faith Feb 1958

As this was a camouflage scheme over high speed silver Allen sprayed the underside with RLM 08 Silber (XA1216). Once the silver was masked off he sprayed Extra Dark Sea Grey (XA1004) and then started masking for the Dark Green (XA1001) using the Blu-Tack sausage method. The kit decals are in excellent register and are incredibly thin - so thin that some stencils wrinkled while applying them to the model but fortunately those that did make it that far settled down really well with no real need for any setting solutions.

### WS103/709 of Station Flight RNAS Yeovilton May 1967

While spraying the colours for WA659 I thought it would be easier to kill two birds with one stone and opted to prime the last model white and spray the red and black at the same time as WA659. After a coat of Klear the decals were applied but I decided that as the majority of the black stencils wouldn't be visible on a black aircraft, I left them off.

## Finishing Touches

Once all the decals had dried we applied another coat of Klear to seal them all. This was followed by a panel line wash of Paynes grey oil paint thinned with pure turpentine. After an hour we wiped the excess off in the direction of airflow. Normally at this point we would seal the weathering by applying a satin or matt varnish but pictures showed these aircraft with a gloss finish so we were happy to leave them at this stage as the weathering had toned the Klear down to a nice scale-effect gloss. Now we were happy with the finishes we

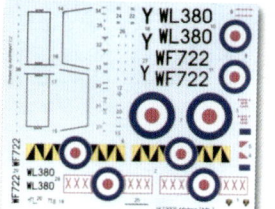

started to attach the undercarriage doors, external fuel tanks and aerials. Finally they were all finished.

## Conclusion

With a little time and patience this kit will build into a nice representation of a twin seat Meteor. Hannants offer a wide range of decals in their Xtradecal range for the Meteor, as well as another Xtrakit of the F.8, and a reboxed upgraded kit of the Matchbox night fighter, and the 'Xtra' product range is certainly one of the first places to go if 1/72 Meteors are on your agenda.

# Chapter 4

**TECH PANEL**

Scale: 1/72

Kit No: A12050

Type: Injection Moulded Plastic

Manufacturer: Airfix

# Hawker Siddely Nimrod

## Building a Better Nimrod

### The BAe Nimrod MR2

By Keith Peckover

The light aperture needs to be extended and the upper part filled. A mask is provided by A2Zee. A lens from little-cars.com was fitted behind the transparency, this also being done with the wing lights

The Hawker Siddeley HS.801, ultimately named Nimrod, was the result of Air Staff Requirement 381 which was issued on 4 June 1964 for a replacement for the by that time ageing Shackleton MR 2. Following a lengthy study of all the available options the intention to order a maritime version of the Comet 4C from Hawker Siddeley under the designation HS 801 was announced in Parliament

**AFTERMARKET ITEMS USED**

Aftermarket Items used:

Alley Cat AC72006C BAe Nimrod Engine Upgrade Set

Alley Cat AC72007C Nimrod Fin, SCP Intake & Nose Wheels

Alley Cat AC72012C Nimrod Windscreen & Mask Set

MasterCasters MST72002 BAe Nimrod Wheels

Xtradecal X72081 BAe Nimrod MR2s and R1

on 2 February 1965.

The HS.801 had the name Nimrod conferred upon it in early 1967 just prior to the prototypes taking to the air for the first time. The two prototype Nimrods, serial numbers XV147 and XV148, were both conversions from civil Comets which were taken from the end of the Comet 4C production line before they were fully completed. XV148 made its maiden flight on 23 May 1967 whilst XV147 made its first flight as a Nimrod on 31 July 1967.

The Airfix Nimrod was a welcome addition to the range of kits available but it has some weak points, which one aftermarket company in particular, A2Zee, has exploited. Three of their sets were used here, and this article aims to illustrate or describe the benefits of

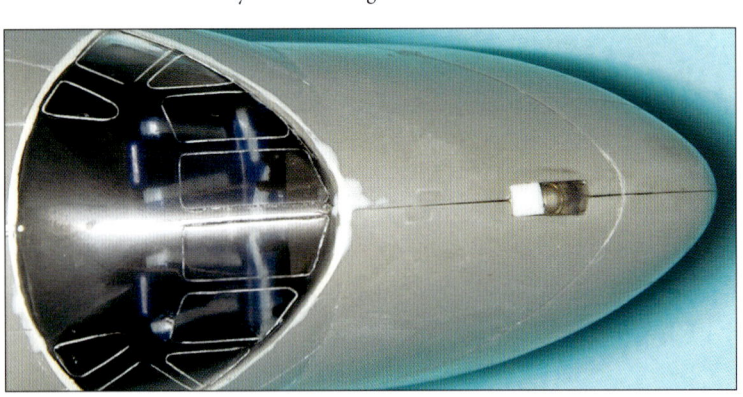

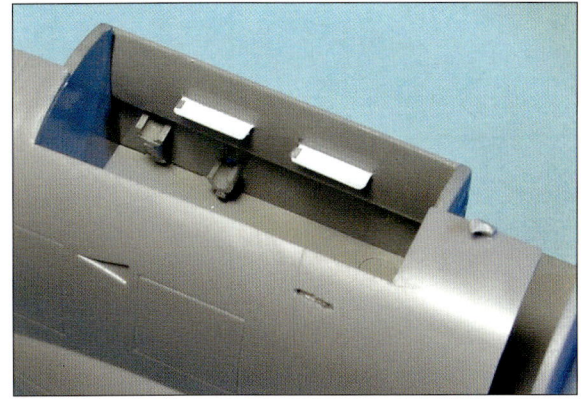

Built from the box the nose gear leg is fixed in place by pins that fit into holes provided in the undercarriage bay side walls, this having to be done when it is assembled. This arrangement was used on one side but on the other the locating pin was removed and the leg supported in the cut-down plastic tubing shown beneath the left hand aerial

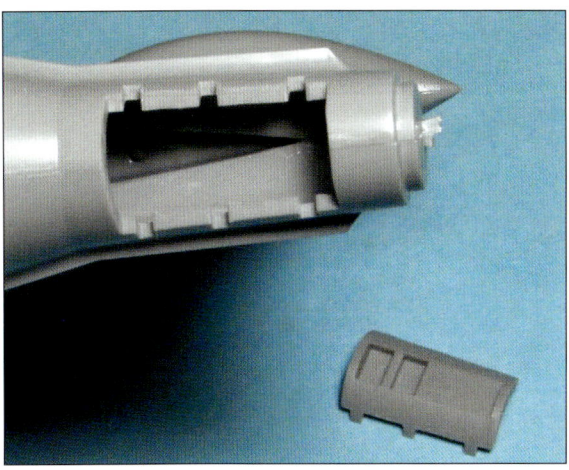

The component not shown in the instructions

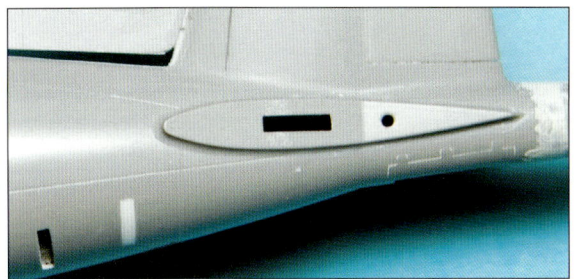

The filled and replacement slots forward of the tailplane and the gap at the base of the replacement fin fillet after it had been fitted

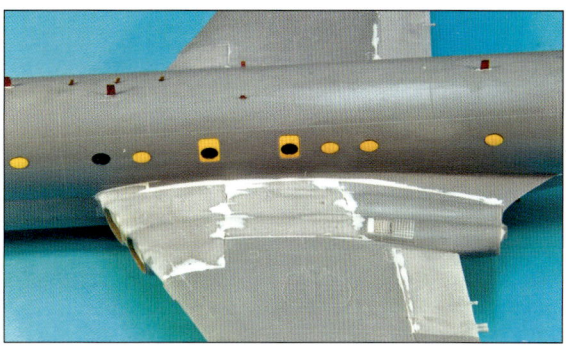

Being blanked off, the second window from the nose is unmasked. It was fitted and sanded flush with the fuselage. The masks that raise the surface of the emergency exits are in place but the window masks are yet to be applied. A sample of the aerial fit is shown. Also presented are the replacement inboard wing sections and flap. An idea of the filling needed may be gained

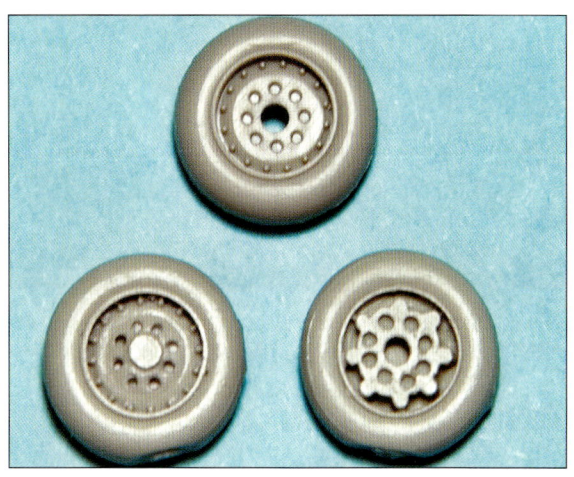

A kit main wheel (top), which is the same on both sides, compared with the MasterCaster replacements. Their set also includes nose wheels and separate spray guards, the latter having the mud flaps absent from the Alley Cat equivalent and consequently being used

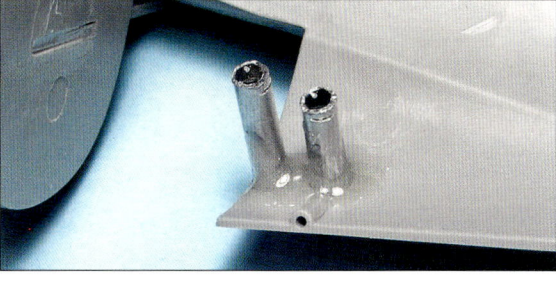

The aluminium tube was secured with 5-minute epoxy resin. Tube was also used to represent an outlet on the underside of the starboard, rear fuselage

the aftermarket sets listed and give an indication of what is involved in building a better Nimrod.

## Construction Notes

Although the build of this kit has been covered in many publications it is worthwhile going over a few points. As moulded, the business end of the in-flight refuelling probe is squared off and needs to be sanded into a hemispherical shape. Remedial work is also required on the nose where the light is too high. The instructions call for the nose undercarriage leg to be fitted at an early stage. It has a weak point, and taking into account the amount of the work to come a change was made to the way it is fitted to enable this to be done late in the build. While working in this area aerials need to be added to the door.

The instructions have some shortcomings. Not covered is the need to blank off one of the port side windows, and the use of a

component is not shown. The appearance required of the recessed areas on this was hard to determine from the photographs available. Suspecting they are covered by transparencies the interior surfaces were painted blue and then 'glazed' with Kristal Klear. The main undercarriage bay outboard doors are shown as being fitted open whereas they should be closed, this being their normal state on the ground unless maintenance work is being undertaken.

A slot adjacent to the port tailplane is too far aft, so was filled with Plasticard and a new one cut. Aluminium tube was used to represent the sonobouy launchers. When fitting the weapons bay roof component it was pressed upwards and glued in place to brace the fuselage in the wing root area.

The kit covers a number of different versions of the Nimrod, some without the wingtip Electronic Support Measures pods. On the kit these covered the outboard end of the ailerons leading me to suspect that the wingtips should have been extended. I adopted the simple

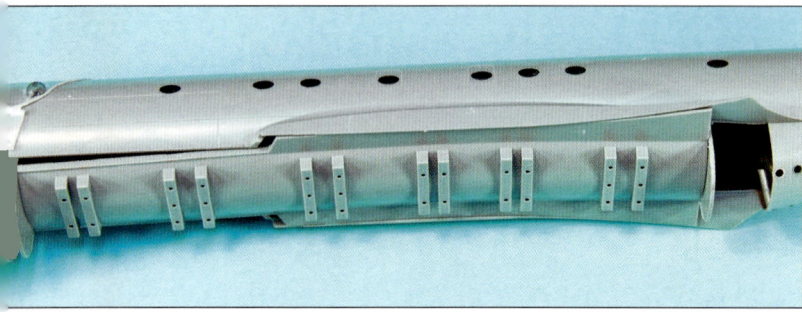

Although securing the roof to the fuselage resulted in it being curved, this was of no matter because the bay doors were to be fitted closed and, in view of work to be done in the wing root area, strengthening the fuselage was of greater importance

The searchlight before the transparency was fitted

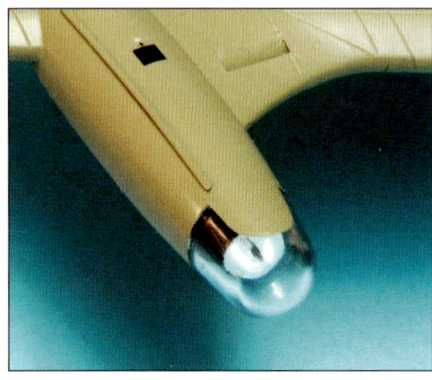

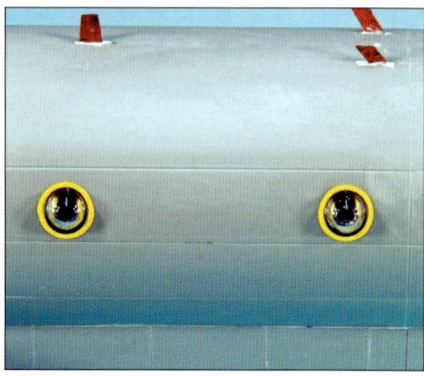

A small amount of work here made a worthwhile enhancement to this area of the model, but its profile is incorrect

Shimming the window components resulted in their exterior face standing just proud of the exit surface

I had doubts about using these rings, fearing that they might look too thick, but they have made a worthwhile improvement to the model's appearance

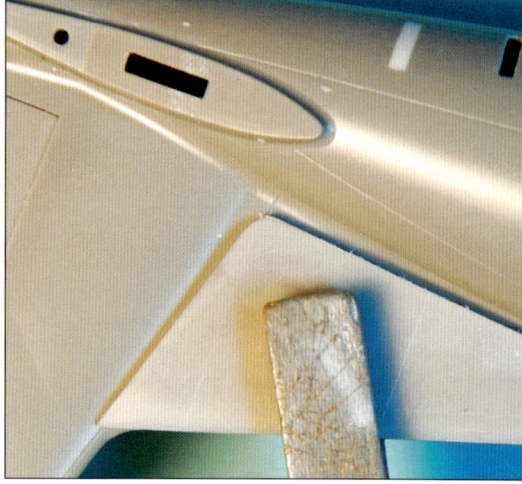

The windscreen and scab plate masks

The finished nose area. The replacement windscreen brings about a significant improvement in the model's accuracy and appearance. The scab plate may just be discerned, being built up of four layers of paint. Etched brass windscreen wipers and the ice probe (beneath the captain's side window) are provided in the Alley Cat set. Forward of the light is the small pointed aerial that was added

With their leading edges aligned, the angle made by the edges of the resin part did not match fuselage and fin

The filling required after the fin fillet was cut away. An incorrectly bulged area was present forward of the pencil line

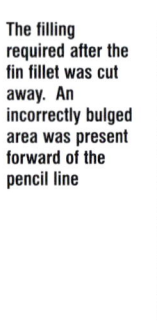

The filling required after the replacement fin fillet was fitted

compromise of engraving a line a little inboard of the pods to denote the aileron's outboard limit and filling the unwanted portion of hinge line beyond this. A hole was drilled in the outboard side of each pod to depict the vent present there. The incorrect size and positioning of the outboard landing lights is corrected by the main Alley Cat set.

To represent the searchlight a piece of Plasticard was dished by pressing it over a spherical surface until it took up the required shape. It was then covered with aluminium foil secured in place with PVA glue. Although not an accurate depiction of the real thing it does give the required impression. What is assumed to be a cable conduit runs along the outboard side of the tank in which the searchlight is fitted. This is missing on the kit and was represented with plastic strip. Regrettably, this area of the model is incorrect because the tank should have a marked reduction in diameter at its interface with the transparency.

When it was too late to do anything about it I noticed that the tailplane finlets are at least twice as thick as they should be.

## Aerials

A small aerial needs to be fitted just above the radome. It has the shape of a tapered spike and was produced by rubbing down a pin on a carborundum stone. Thin sheet metal superglued into slots cut into the fuselage was used to represent blade aerials. This approach results in their having a realistic thickness and they are damage tolerant compared with just attaching them to the surface at the end of the build.

## Exits, Windows & Windscreen (set AC72012C)

The emergency exits are, quite correctly, recessed but excessively so. This results in the transparencies standing well above the exit surface. To avoid having to reduce their thickness by sanding them down they were shimmed with Plasticard. The excessive depth is addressed by the means of masks that remain in place after painting. These are specific to each site because there is a slight variation in exit dimensions. To represent the reinforcing rings fitted around the observation domes, masks are provided which again remain in place. A reservation over the use of masks in this way is the fear that they may come unstuck at some time in the future.

To fit the transparent resin replacement windscreen the upper fuselage aft of the flight deck has to be shimmed with 20 thou Plasticard to increase its width. Whether this is required because the fuselage is too narrow or the resin part too wide is not known. With the fuselage having been assembled before the set was obtained (it came on the market after work had started) the joint had to be opened up with a razor saw.

The Nimrod's windscreen is reinforced with a scab plate that encompasses its entire area. This is a subtle feature that is difficult to represent satisfactorily by gluing on Plasticard. Alley Cat have addressed this by providing paint masks to outline the plate. Paint is built up within the area defined by the masks forming a raised

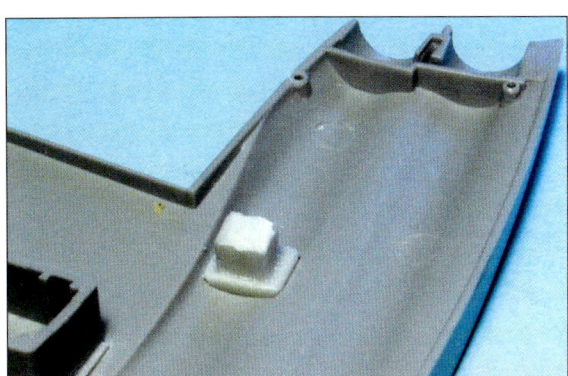

Retaining the casting risers provided a convenient means of handling the cascades during fitting. Test fits were mainly carried out from below. After the cascades were fixed in place the risers were cut off to enable the wings to be joined

Replacement rear fuselage air intake compared with the undersize kit part

section. This, combined with the correct window shapes, makes a significant improvement to the model's appearance.

## Replacing the fin fillet (set AC72007C)

The kit's fin fillet is about twice as thick as it should be and has a tapered rather than flat cross section. I assumed it would be just be a case of cutting this part away and attaching A2Zee's replacement but this was not so. After the kit's fillet was removed the resulting gaps were filled with Plasticard and superglue. When doing this it was realised that the contour of the forward region of the fin was bulged instead of being a natural extension of its profile and required sanding down.

The position on the fin's leading edge at which to fix the upper point of the new fillet was determined by reference to photos and drawings. The shortest side of the fillet was then adjusted to obtain the required angle between fin and fillet leading edges. After fitting a tapered gap was present at the base of the fillet that was filled with Plasticard, and Milliput then used to blend it with fuselage and fin.

I suspect that the point at which the leading edge of the new part meets the fuselage is slightly too far forward and have since read that the fin chord is 3 - 4mm oversize. This did not come as a surprise because, albeit judged against photos, doubts had arisen over its accuracy, not only regarding this aspect but its thickness which seemed to be too great.

This kit also has a replacement intake for the rear fuselage.

## Thrust Reversers (set AC72006C)

The cascades are finely cast and liable to damage during fitting, although this is avoidable by retaining their casting risers. The kit cascade engravings are incorrectly positioned, the replacement underside units go rearwards and the upper units forward. The holes I cut in the top of the nacelles were located slightly too far forward because, forgetting advice in Alley Cat's instructions and using a photo as guidance, they were positioned with respect to the flap hinge. In so doing the reason replacement inboard flaps are provided was overlooked, this being that the chord of the kit's inboard flaps is too great and as a consequence their hinge line too far forward.

## Replacing the Inboard Wing

This is where the bulk of set AC72006C is used. The first task was to paint the interior of the intake ducts. A2Zee recommend that to fit the engine compressor faces (not turbine blades as they call them - wrong end of the engine, guys!) the intake ducts may need to be reamed slightly. However, they fell into place and had to be mounted on Plasticard backing plates.

Major surgery is required to fit the replacement intake and engine cover sections. The easiest job is cutting away the forward section of the wing root moulded with the fuselage. Alley Cat imply

The upper cascade and Plasticard filler required due to the hole having been cut in the wrong place. No harm done, just extra work. Alley Cat advise that the cascades should lie just below the nacelle surface. The superiority of these parts compared with the engraved lines on the kit, albeit here they have been filled, is evident

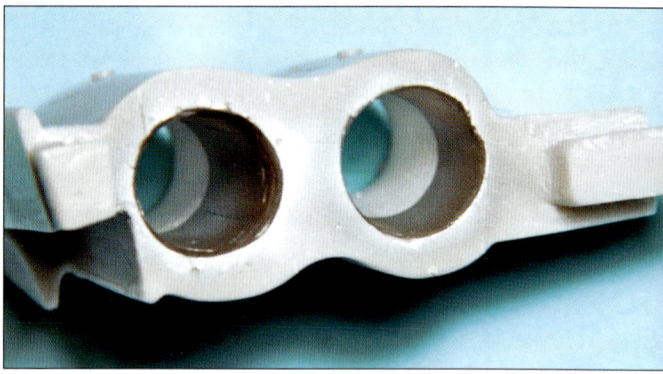

After the forward section of the intake ducts had been sprayed white the natural metal portion was represented using decal trim film

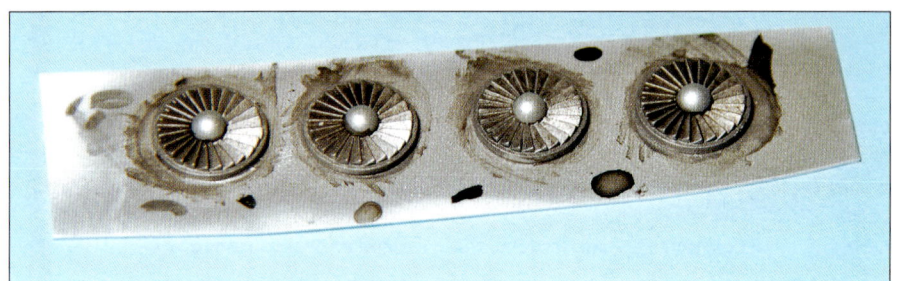

The compressor faces before their backing plates were cut down

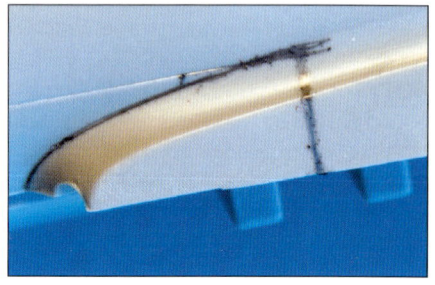

The forward end of the wing root has to be cut away

It was found that alignment of the nacelles was considerably better on the upper surface than below

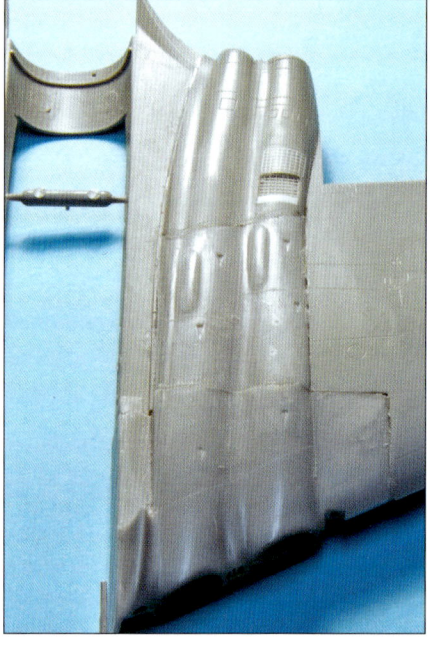

The wing root was in a reasonably straight line

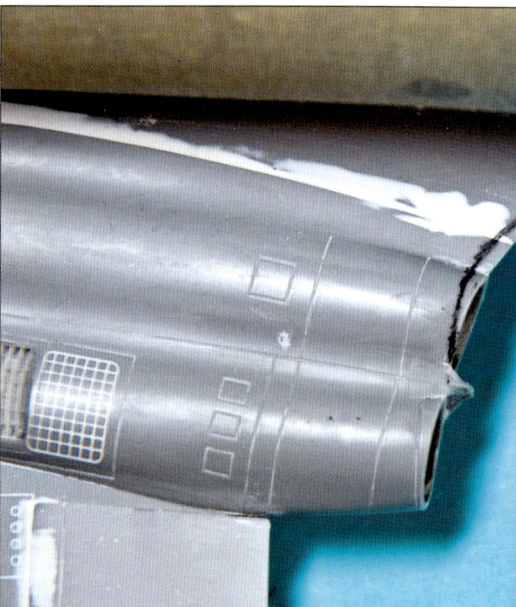

Viewed in plan the aft edge of the nacelles should be in a straight line and the root trailing edge reprofiled as indicated

Kit, outboard, and Alley Cat, inboard, jet pipes compared. With a little sanding to taper their profile the kit parts look closer to the real thing

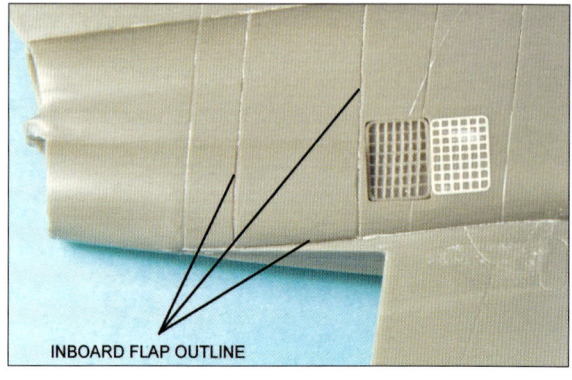

INBOARD FLAP OUTLINE

There are no panel lines on the kit to denote the under-nacelle flap sections so a little scribing is needed

that the new parts are to be fitted before the top and bottom of the wings are joined but I elected to fix them together and believe this to have been beneficial.

The particular challenge seen was that of aligning the nacelles across three sections (ie original tailpipe segment, replacement engine cover and intakes) whilst at the same time keeping the wing root in a straight line. Dozens of test fits were necessary, indeed essential, including wing to fuselage, and during this it was realized that it was best not to glue the top and bottom wing sections at the root, something that fortunately had not been done.

The approach taken was to fit the engine cover first. Its joint line on the kit was sanded back until the new intake section was basically aligned with the wing leading edge and the resin flash trimmed down until the nacelle sat at the correct height above the wing. The leading edge of the replacement intake was left slightly proud of the kit's wing, believing it better to have to sand it back a little after assembly had been completed than to apply filler. The cover was initially fixed in place with 5-minute epoxy applied only to its joint with the tailpipe area. It was held in alignment with the outboard wing while the epoxy set, and when this had been done a test fit to check how the wing root looked was made. Having established that this was satisfactory superglue was used along its joint with the wing.

The intake section was then fixed in place, alignment being something of an issue. Joints were then filled and sanded, bringing most work on this part of the build to a welcome but not complete end because Alley Cat draw attention to the incorrect profile of the nacelle tail pipe area.

A2Zee's jet pipes were not used. They would have required the removal of strengthening webs within the nacelles plus thinning of the walls. This area of the kit was being affected enough as it was so I preferred to leave it alone. Furthermore, when comparing them with photos of the real thing the conclusion was drawn that the kit parts were better.

The work required on the flaps is largely due to the chord of the kit flaps being too great, particularly the inboard unit, and as a result its hinge line is too far forward and the trailing edge shape incorrect.

## Painting and decaling

Xtracolor enamels were used and after decaling the model was sprayed with Humbrol satin varnish. When the kit was released its decal sheet was the subject of adverse criticism and an examination

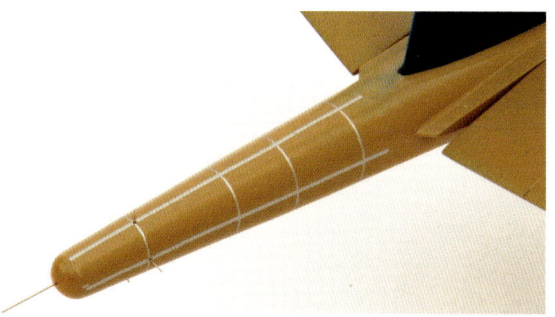

Not to be forgotten are the spikes on the MAD boom. The engraved lines on the boom were filled. Why were they there in the first place?

of it resulted in the purchase of Xtradecal X72081. On seeing XZ284 in 206 Squadron's 80th anniversary markings with its roundel-blue fin, conspicuous white numbers and octopus, the other options stood no chance of being selected. The decals were of excellent quality, easily positioned and showed no sign of silvering. Most importantly there was no colour bleed-through on the numbers, this being checked beforehand by a test with a white lightning flash belonging to another option.

Only a limited number of the kit stencil decals were applied, my approach being that if I cannot see them in real life when the aircraft has the same apparent size as the model in front of me they don't go on. Some showed a tendency to silver even though they were laid over a film of Micro Set on a surface of gloss varnish.

Final tasks consisted of fixing in place the MAD probe 'spikes', etched brass wiper blades and ice probe, and rigging the wire aerials using elasticized thread by Aeroclub.

## Conclusions

The incorporation of these resin sets obviously results in a significant increase in cost, work and build time. Some may think their use an extravagance and the sharp eyed may notice that the shape of the replacement engine intakes is somewhat suspect. Notwithstanding the latter, I feel the overall improvement in accuracy and appearance brought about to be more than sufficient justification.

43

**Nimrod MR.1 XV257**
Seen in its early over water colours of light aircraft grey over white, black serials and roundels in six positions

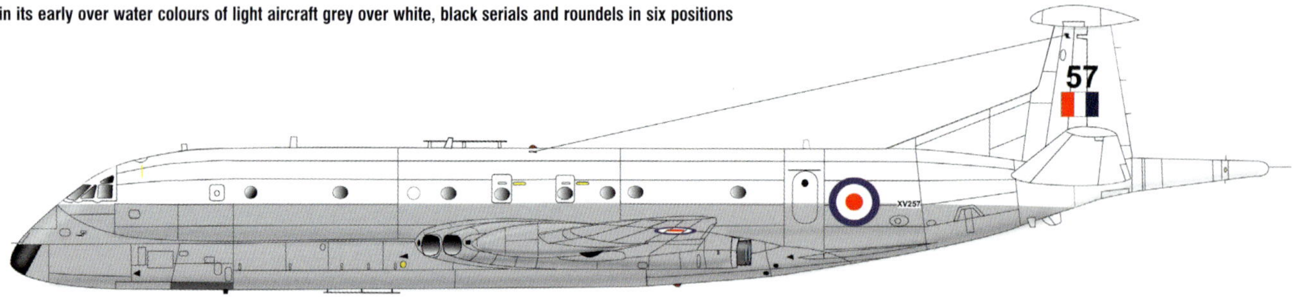

**Nimrod AEW.3 Prototype XZ286**
Based at RAF Waddington in July 1980 for initial trials work. The aircraft is painted Light aircraft grey on its lower fuselage and wings with white applied to the upper surfaces, fin and rudder. The serials are in black with red, white and blue roundels in six positions. Note the nose and tail fairings which were in some cases unpainted, thus having a buff colouring

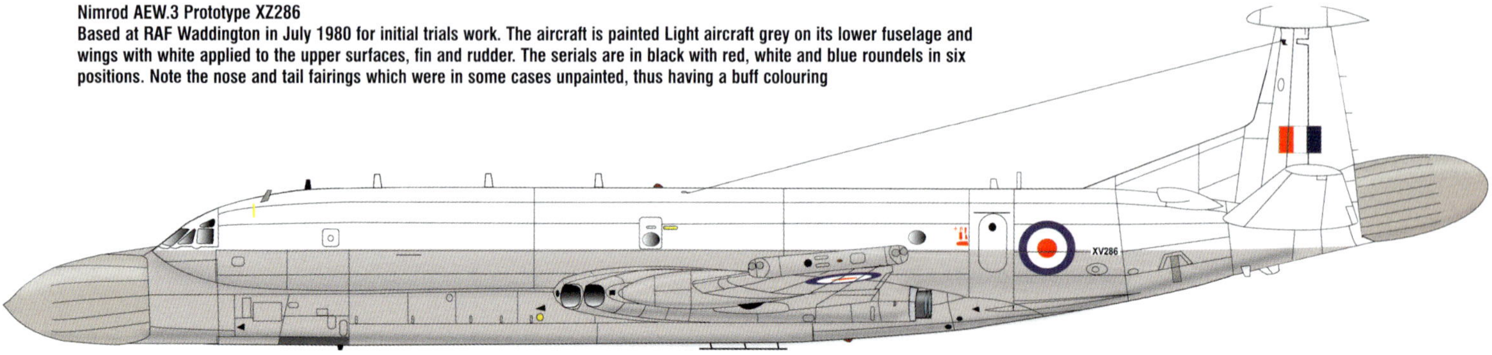

**Nimrod MR.2P XV244 'Battlestar'**
No.42 Squadron RAF Kinloss Wings based at Seeb in Oman during the 1992 Gulf War. Serials are in black, with pale pink and pale blue roundels in six positions. The aircraft is painted in the standard Hemp and Light Aircraft grey scheme and carries fourteen mission symbols and four ship silhouettes. Although not illustrated here, the aircraft was also able to carry Tornado style BOZ-107 chaff and flare dispensers

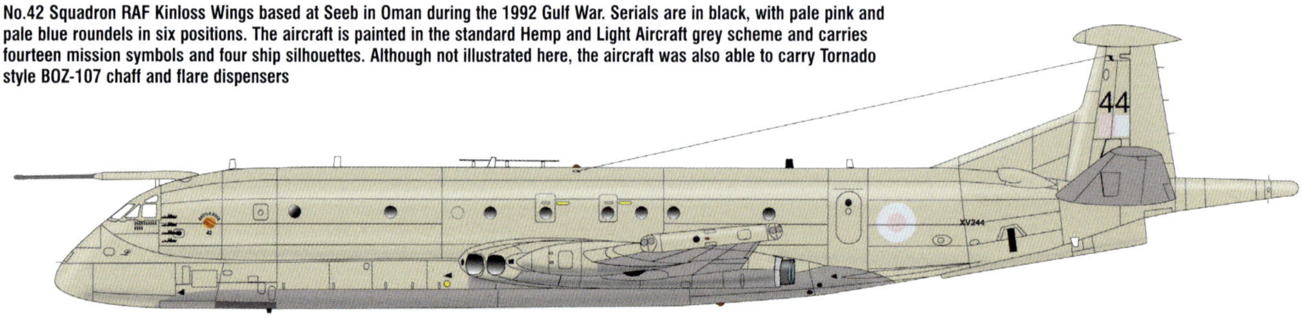

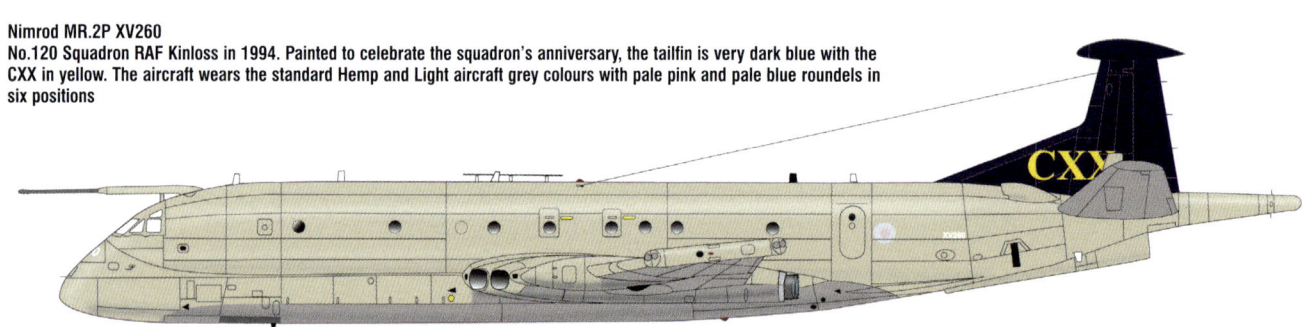

**Nimrod MR.2P XV260**
No.120 Squadron RAF Kinloss in 1994. Painted to celebrate the squadron's anniversary, the tailfin is very dark blue with the CXX in yellow. The aircraft wears the standard Hemp and Light aircraft grey colours with pale pink and pale blue roundels in six positions

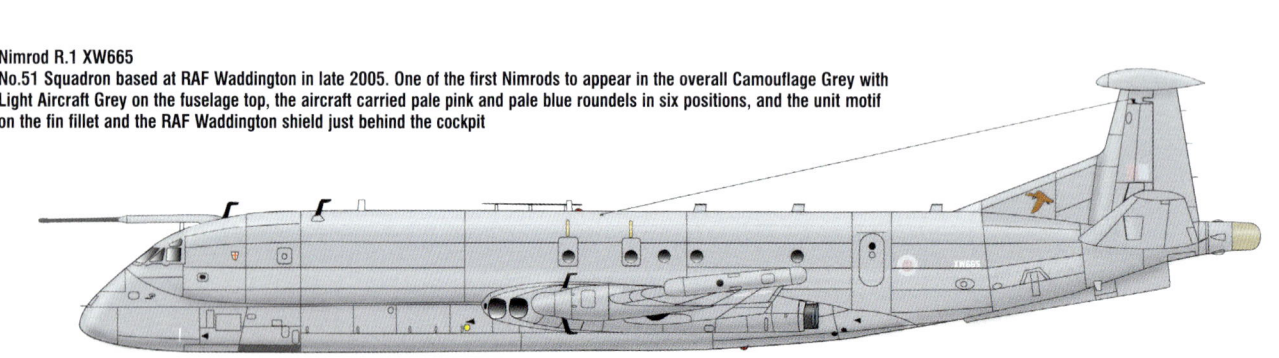

**Nimrod R.1 XW665**
No.51 Squadron based at RAF Waddington in late 2005. One of the first Nimrods to appear in the overall Camouflage Grey with Light Aircraft Grey on the fuselage top, the aircraft carried pale pink and pale blue roundels in six positions, and the unit motif on the fin fillet and the RAF Waddington shield just behind the cockpit

**Nimrod MR.2**

Top & Bottom views. The Nimrod MR.2 shown here carries the Falklands refuelling probe fit but has yet to acquire the wing tip mounted Yellowgate ESM pods. The aircraft was also outfitted for the carriage of Sidewinder missiles as necessary. The standard camouflage scheme of Help and Light Aircraft Grey has now been applied; however the roundels remain high visibility blue and red

45

# Accessorize – Nimrod AEW.3

## A Conversion Parts Review

By Andy McCabe

With the retirement of the rapidly ageing Avro Shackleton the RAF was seeking a replacement for its Airborne Early Warning (AEW) fleet. The BAe Nimrod, already in service, was chosen as the airframe to be converted and development work duly commenced. The modifications were not subtle externally and two huge radomes were fitted to house the large GEC Marconi Radars, giving the aircraft rather bulbous tail and nose cones.

The project was to be plagued with problems throughout its design, build, testing and service life, and as early as the first test flight in 1982 difficulties were encountered. The problems and cost overruns with the GEC 4080M computer used for the Mission System Avionics were increasingly leading the MoD to the conclusion that the project might not entirely fulfil the role it was intended to perform and the project was cancelled in 1986 and the Boeing E-3 Sentry ordered in its place; the order however was not accepted until 1988.

This would have left the UK without any AEW Capability until the deliveries of the E-3 Sentry could commence and this was not to be until 1991, so the Government was forced to convert 12 obsolete Shackleton MR.2s into interim AEW aircraft until the Sentry arrived.

The Nimrod AEW aircraft was, as are the majority of development projects, subjected to constant design, role and system changes

| PARTS USED |
|---|
| Airfix #12050 BAe Nimrod MR 1/MR 2/MR 2P/R 1 |
| Cammett AEW3 Nimrod Conversion for Airfix Kit |
| Alley Cat #AC72006C Nimrod Engine Upgrade Set for Airfix kit |

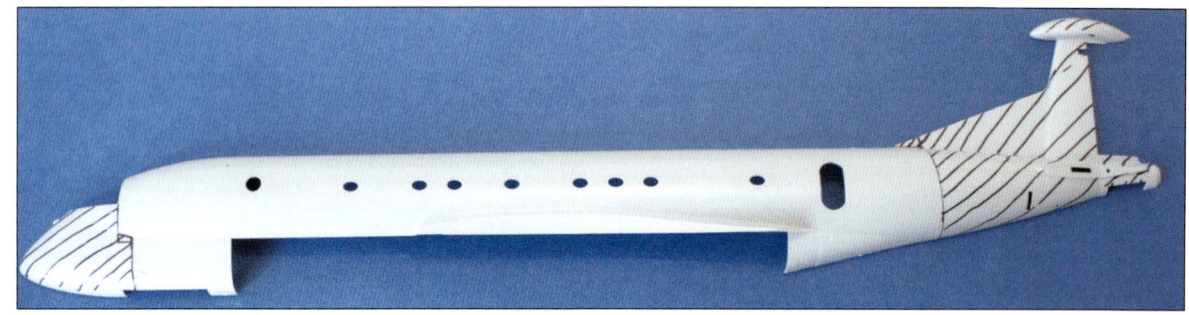

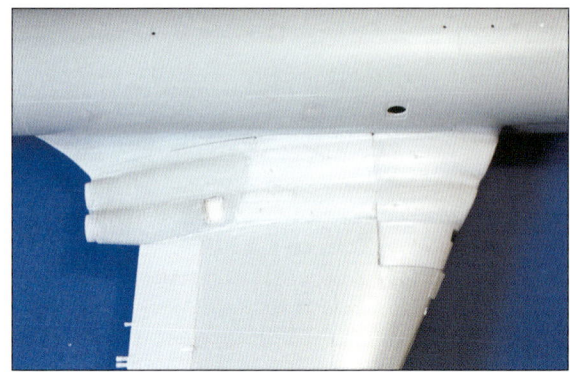

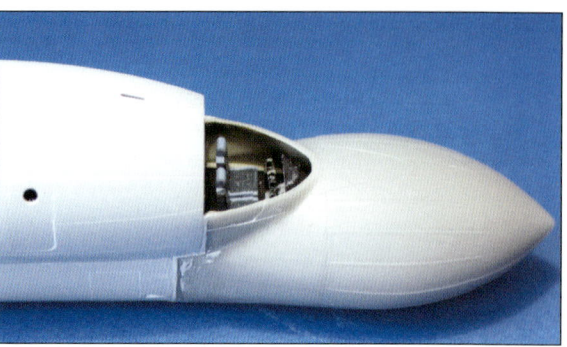

throughout its development and it is therefore probable that the failure to meet its remit was not entirely down to the aircraft or its systems and more to the constant changes heaped upon it.

I had always liked the look of the Nimrod AEW.3, so the release by Cammett of an upgrade kit caught my eye straight away. This particular kit consists of replacement nose and tail radar bulges in solid resin, replacement vertical tail and rudder, and horizontal tailplanes. I had also spied an engine upgrade by Alley Cat that provided the correct seamless engine intakes, so a set was duly purchased ready for a rather large lot of kit bashing.

## Construction

It is quite a step actually to cut up a perfectly good model kit for no other reason than to satisfy a whim, so with a large gulp the razor saw went into action. The nose and tail sections from the fuselage were cut away from both fuselage halves. Cammett have designed their resin replacement parts to coincide with panel lines on the Airfix kit parts so the locations of the cut lines are well defined.

Other modifications to the fuselage parts include blanking off

certain window openings, and these are shown on the instructions but it is also wise to check references such as the excellent publication by Andy Evans on the Nimrod. The cockpit floor also requires modification by cutting back until it is level with the forward edge of the instrument panel.

The nose and tail replacement parts are made of solid resin and are quite weighty components, especially the tail section, which along with the tailplane and vertical tail parts means that a considerable amount of extra nose weight will be required. Cammett reckon an extra 75gm. I added 80gm and yet it still needed more at the end as I had a tail sitter, so I fed another 10gm through the cabin windows before they were filled with Micro Kristal Klear.

Once the two fuselage halves were joined the cut lines for the replacement nose and tail were carefully sanded back with a sanding stick until the parts fitted perfectly to the fuselage, and were then superglued into position. The fit of the replacement nose and tail is superb so long as it is done gently without taking huge amounts out of the plastic parts.

The remainder of the Cammett kit parts were test fitted then put back into the box for fitting later on.

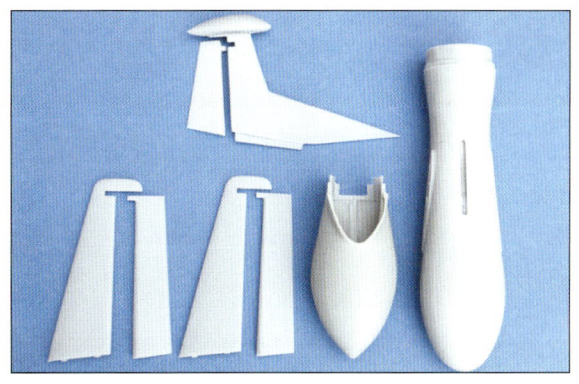

The next stage involved removing even more of the Airfix plastic as it was time to start work on the wings. Each wing half (upper and lower) was measured and marked according to the Alley Cat instructions, then the sections cut and sanded back to a point roughly close to the marked lines. The wing halves were taped together and the cut lines were finally sanded back until the resin intake part was a nice tight fit, and once achieved the upper engine casing section of the plastic wing was marked and cut out ready for the resin replacement.

Other modifications to the Nimrod wing include new resin thrust reversers, which are located in different positions to those marked on the Airfix kit wings, longer jet pipes, and correct profile inner wing flaps.

The trailing inner edges of the wings need reprofiling to a flatter rather than curved profile before the jet pipes are installed.

The wing root on each half of the fuselage also has to be removed as the new resin intakes have a reprofiled section moulded into them, again do this carefully so that too much is not removed.

With the major bits removed from the kit's wings assembly can

begin. The kit's engine fan blades are used, and these were glued to the new resin intakes though not until the intakes were sprayed gloss white.

The plastic wing halves were now glued together and allowed to thoroughly dry. The lower half of the fuselage fairing around the munitions bay needs modifying due to the new resin intakes, and after this was fitted the wing assembly was glued into place, starting from the rear underside and working forward leaving the upper joints until the resin parts had been installed and glued into place. The whole lot was then firmly fixed together.

The vertical resin tail, rudder and horizontal tailplanes could now be fitted and lined up to make sure that everything is square. These parts are from the Cammett set and fit perfectly to the new tail section.

The AEW.3 has various antennae along the dorsal spine which are supplied in the standard Nimrod kit though not necessarily in the positions shown in the Airfix instructions, so the correct locations were gleaned from various photos, and the refuelling probe was fitted at this point as well.

47

At this stage the aircraft was sprayed with a coat of primer followed by a coat of Xtrarylix RAF Light Aircraft Grey to the undersurfaces. When dry the demarcation between the upper and lower colours was masked off and Xtracrylix Hemp was applied to the upper surfaces.

There are no decals in the Airfix kit that provide serial numbers for the AEW versions but Model Alliance have recently released a sheet for the Nimrod AEW. I made my own serial numbers along with the roundels and tail bars as the Airfix roundels appeared slightly out of register. Once the decals had been applied a coat of Johnson's Klear was sprayed over to seal them into place and a dark dirt wash was applied to highlight the panel lines, followed by another coat of Klear.

## Conclusion

This was a complex and comprehensive build that entailed a large amount of cutting away of the Airfix kit, but what a result! For all the comments about the ugliness of the Nimrod AEW.3 I actually think the opposite. The Cammett resin parts are very cleanly cast and are superbly made, as are the Alley Cat engine replacements. Careful attention needs to be paid to both sets of instructions to ensure that the parts fit as they are intended, but the end result is awesome and will look good sat next to the Airfix Sentry.

# Chapter 5

# Harrier
## Modelling a 'Mud Mover'

### Harrier GR 3 in the South Atlantic

By Neil Robinson

Little introduction is needed for the Harrier, but with the aircraft now retired from British service, the early years of its service are fading into memory, The often quoted Harrier phrase that it 'couldn't carry a matchbox across a football field' has in many ways exemplified just how wrong that speaker was and just how potent an aircraft the Harrier became in fulfilling its promise as a 'jump-jet'.

Both the Harrier GR 3 and Sea Harrier FRS 1 kits by Airfix originally date back a good few years – 1983 for the Sea Harrier and 1984/5 for the Harrier GR 3 – and had no additional work done to the moulds when they were re-released, (for the 20th Annivesary of the Falklands War), in early 2002, as illustrated by the minimal cockpit interior

detailing and raised panel lines. However, both are still generally accurate models and provide a good basis for acceptable replicas – with a little additional detailing.

Construction began with the cockpit interior – and it really does require some additional detail adding – in my case by using the old Airwaves etched brass accessory sets AC48084, (which is suitable for both the Sea Harrier FRS 1 and Harrier GR 3).

The Harrier/Sea Harrier cockpit interiors were Admiralty Grey overall, a light/medium grey shade, for which I used Humbrol 165 Sea Grey Medium with various switches and panels and the control column hand grip picked out in black. I used the kit instrument panel and side console decals which are adequate as not a great deal can be seen inside the cockpit once the fuselage halves are joined.

I replaced the kit's ejection seat with an Aeroclub white-metal Martin Baker Mk 9B ejection sea, EJ406. Not only is it much more detailed than the kit item – it is heavier which helps to weight the nose. The seat was painted very dark grey with a black head box. When dry, Silver 'Rub n Buff', (a metal paste), was rubbed on, using a lint free cloth, to add some authentic looking wear. The seat cushion, back pad and the head rest were painted various olive/green shades and the etched brass straps, (from the Airwaves accessory set, AC48084), painted blue and tan, were added.

Before I joined the fuselage halves, the back plates for the exhaust nozzles were glued into place and the three-part Pegasus engine front painted matt black with the impeller blades picked out in silver 'Rub n Buff', was fitted.

Heritage Aviation market a series of Harrier/Sea Harrier resin accessory sets, which include intake fronts with drooped auxiliary blow-in doors, white-metal undercarriage legs and resin main and nose wheels, replacement exhaust nozzles and replacement tailplanes with end plates – all of which fit both Airfix kits with very little effort – and when used, certainly do make a noticeable difference.

After the wing halves were assembled and attached to the fuselage, the wing-to-fuselage joins were rubbed down and the fuselage/wing contours blended together. This removed much of the raised detail which had to be rescribed, and whilst I was at it, I also rescribed many of the other raised panel lines, especially on the upper surfaces of wings across the mid fuselage section and the flap lines, and added some further detail using thin plastic card.

A missing intake – the small rear-facing one in front of the starboard gas turbine starter/auxiliary power unit grille – was added, fashioned from a suitable diameter length of sprue, sanded to shape. Thankfully the fit of the wings to the fuselage is good and accurately sets the marked anhedral typical of the Harrier/Sea Harrier. Whilst I was emphasising the separation between the ailerons and flaps by razor cutting from the trailing edge, I also added the fuel jettison pipes from thin plastic tube. I also cut out the wing-tip navigation lights and fitted clear plastic sprue in to the vacant rectangles, which I later sanded to shape and brought back to clarity using Johnsons 'Klear'.

### The 'Blue Eric' ECM fit

The kit's 30mm ADEN cannon pods were improved, initially by drilling out the front ends and fitting a thin plastic tube for the 30mm cannon barrel which protruded slightly. However, I then realised I needed to represent the 'Blue Eric' Electronic Counter Measures unit fitted in the starboard gun pod, which appears to have been carried by all the Harrier GR 3s that operated off Hermes during the Falklands War.

Basically, the components from a Sky Shadow ECM jammer were modified and fitted inside the starboard 30mm ADEN cannon pod which had been emptied of the cannon and ammunition. On my model, this was represented by a small rectangle of plastic card, glued to the forward outer side of the starboard gun pod, just in front of the cannon case ejection chute fairing, to represent the air intake to cool the equipment.

This was painted a slightly 'fresher' Dark Green to represent a newly fitted piece of equipment. Then the previously opened starboard cannon barrel needed a 'plug' to represent the domed fairing fitted in place of the 30mm cannon barrel, which was shaped from suitable diameter plastic rod and painted a very dark grey. In the event, the 'Blue Eric' ECM jammer, (named after Sqn Ldr Eric Annal, an electronic engineering officer working at the Ministry of Defence at the time), wasn't used in action.

On the Harrier GR 3, the camera port is on the port side, (only indicated by raised lines on the kit), so this was drilled out and glazed. An I-Band Transponder, which helped the Harriers to be positively identified on the British ships' radar – when it worked! – was fitted under the GR 3's Laser Ranger and Marked Target Seeker (LRMTS) nose, in the form of an oblong fairing with a blade aerial in the middle. I made the fairing from laminations of plastic card faired-in with filler and the aerial from thin plastic card.

The main and nose undercarriage legs and wheel hubs were painted gloss Light Aircraft Grey. Wheel well bay interiors and the insides of the undercarriage doors were also painted Light Aircraft Grey, and then 'dirtied-up' to try and hide the lack of detail! When the aircraft was 'at rest', the nose and mainwheel doors were invariably 'open' – however if the aircraft was 'under power' they were generally closed, primarily to avoid any ingestation of FOD. The inside face of the ventral airbrake, which also drooped open when the aircraft was 'at rest', was Dark Sea Grey.

One of the 'casualties' of using common sprues for both the Sea Harrier/Harrier kits, is that the ventral air brake on the Harrier GR 3 is too small. Ideally, the air brake bay needs enlarging and the air brake extending in length. I cheated here and 'borrowed' an air brake from a scrapped Monogram AV-8B kit, which is the correct size, and quietly ignored the size of the bay. Ahem!

### Falklands War scheme

I decided to finish my Harrier GR 3 as XZ997/31, as she looked on 28 May 1982, when, as one of three aircraft that took part in the three-aircraft attack on Argentinean gun positions at Goose Green that were holding up the 2 Para's assault on the settlement. Piloted by Flt Lt Tony Harper, in company with Sqn Ldrs Jerry Pook and Peter Harris in XV789/32 and XZ989/07 respectively, and armed with Royal Navy 2 inch rocket pods, the text-book attack helped to convince the Argentineans to surrender on the following morning.

You might be excused for expecting to find the standard RAF 68mm SNEB rocket pods in with the Airfix Harrier GR 3 kit, but in fact there are four Royal Navy 2 inch rocket pods included, (parts 63 to 74) – fortuitously for me! They appear to have had pale grey frangible-head nose cones, bright silver/natural metal main bodies and dark gun-metal coloured rear sections, which is how I painted the pair I fitted to my model.

The wraparound camouflage scheme was applied using Humbrol 164 Dark Sea Grey and 163 Dark Green. A bit of judicious post-shading, plus various panels picked out in Xtracolor Dark Sea Grey and Black Green, gave the model a well-used 'operational' look – especially noticeable on the small access panels on the upper surface of the wings – seen on several photographs taken during the conflict. A final top coat of semi-matt varnish was applied to blend the decals and paintwork in.

The markings were mainly straight from the Airfix kit, the only item not from the Airfix kit being the red fin top numeral '31' which came from Aztec sheet 48-016 *All Harriers*, which offers markings for nine of the Falklands War Harrier GR 3s to be modelled.

**Note**: XZ997/31 was used on numerous sorties during the Falklands War, (flown by various pilots), including attacks on Stanley Airport and also took part in the first successful 1000lb Laser Guided Bomb (LGB) attack on 13 June, against Argentinean positions on Tumbledown, flown by W/Cdr Peter Squire.

# Falklands Bomber

## The ESCI 1/72 Harrier GR 3 kit in Falklands War markings

By Jan Forsgren

ESCI produced lots of excellent kits in the 1980s and this Harrier, from this era, is no exception, with nice surface detail and neatly recessed panel lines, but the cockpit needs extra detailing.

The kit was easy to build and not much filler was needed in the seams. I remember thinking how easy it was compared to the kits I had built decades before. I replaced the kit seat with an Aeroclub white metal Martin Baker ejection seat.

It was painted with Xtracolor Dark Green and Dark Sea Grey wraparound camouflage; the masking was done with ordinary drafting tape which was cut with a sharp knife.

All the decals used were provided in the kit, and sealed in with acrylic gloss and satin varnishes. The only weathering was the exhaust stain on the fuselage behind the engine exhaust, heavily applied, using black pastel chalk.

### RAF HARRIER GR 3S USED IN OPERATION CORPORATE

BAe Harrier GR 3 XV762, of 233 OCU Wittering, transferred to No 1(F) Sqn, allocated code 37 . ALE-40 chaff/IR flare dispensers fitted.

BAe Harrier GR 3 XV778, coded 16 of No 1(F) Sqn. ALE-40 chaff/IR flare dispensers and Blue Eric ECM fitted.

BAe Harrier GR 3 XV787, coded 02 of No 1(F) Sqn. ALE-40 not fitted.

BAe Harrier GR 3 XV789 of No IV(AC) Sqn, Gutersloh. Transferred to No 1(F) Sqn, allocated code 32 . ALE-40 not fitted. SQN LDR FISHER in black under starboard windscreen.

BAe Harrier GR 3 XW767, coded 06 of No 1(F) Sqn. ALE-40 chaff/IR flare dispensers fitted.

BAe Harrier GR 3 XW919, coded 03 of No 1(F) Sqn. ALE-40 chaff/IR flare dispensers and Blue Eric ECM fitted.

BAe Harrier GR 3 XW924, of 233 OCU Wittering. Transferred to No 1(F) Sqn, allocated code 35 . ALE-40 chaff/IR flare dispensers fitted.

BAe Harrier GR 3 XZ129, coded 29 of No 1(F) Sqn. ALE-40 chaff/IR flare dispensers fitted.

BAe Harrier GR 3 XZ132, of 233 OCU Wittering, transferred to No 1(F) Sqn, allocated code 36 . ALE-40 chaff/IR flare dispensers fitted.

BAe Harrier GR 3 XZ133, of 233 OCU Wittering, transferred to No 1(F) Sqn, allocated code 10 . ALE-40 chaff/IR flare dispensers and Blue Eric ECM fitted.

BAe Harrier GR 3 XZ963, coded 14 of No 1(F) Sqn. ALE-40 not fitted.

BAe Harrier GR 3 XZ972, of 233 OCU Wittering, transferred to No 1(F) Sqn, allocated code 33 . ALE-40 not fitted.

BAe Harrier GR 3 XZ988, of 233 OCU Wittering, transferred to No 1(F) Sqn, allocated code 34 . ALE-40 chaff/IR flare dispensers fitted.

BAe Harrier GR 3 XZ989, coded 07 of No 1(F) Sqn. ALE-40 not fitted.

BAe Harrier GR 3 XZ992, coded 05 of No 1(F) Sqn. ALE-40 chaff/IR flare dispensers fitted.

BAe Harrier GR 3 XZ997, of IV(AC) Sqn, Gutersloh, transferred to No 1(F) Sqn, allocated code 31 . ALE-40 not fitted.

A great view of the GR.3 with a SNEB launcher on its outer wing pylon

# '2, 3 and 4' Harriers at Wittering

**A**llan J Harper delves into his archive and provides a photographic look at the latter days of the RAF's first generation Harriers, both single and two-seaters, at RAF Wittering.

RAF Wittering was for many years the 'Home of the Harrier', and I was privileged on a number of occasions to be able to visit the base, and photograph its aircraft, in particular, the latter days of the GR 3, and the T 2 and T 4 respectively, as they were at this time on the verge of being superseded by the much more powerful GR 5 and GR 7, and some time later by the T 10. The photographs here also go to prove that the British weather is no respecter of the aviation enthusiast, as during at least two visits, it was either grey overcast, raining or indeed closed-in with a grey mist! But, these things are sent to try us, and thanks to the settings of the trusty SLR camera, something useful was achieved, in that images of the older versions of the Harrier could be captured, and enjoyed well after the type has been retired.

The ubiquitous 'step ladders' needed to access the two-seat Harrier are evident here, and are needed due to the lack of internal steps

Harrier GR.3 XZ971/3A, waits for its next occupant

The taller tail fin and longer rear fuselage of the two-seat Harrier

The shape of things to come! A Harrier GR.3 frames three GR 5s

Harrier GR.3 XV753/3F of No.233 OCU. The letter on the tailcode denotes that this was a GR.3, as some GR 5's with single-letter tail codes were just beginning to appear

Harrier XZ998/3F carries no squadron insignia at this time

A good view up over the rear of a Harrier T 4. Note the disparity between the tail code and the code on the outrigger wheels

Harrier GR.3 ZD670/3C now in the markings of No.4 Squadron, was now serving with No.233 OCU, and had also seen service with 1453 Flight in the Falkland Islands

With its Pegasus engine running, the pilot has a quick word with the groundcrew before taxiing. Note the separate canopy and windshield separating the cockpits

Harrier T 4 XW271/X in the colour of No.3 Squadron, but on strength with No.233 OCU during the early 1990s

A rather grey scene, but brightened by T 4 ZB603, which was later passed to the Royal Navy for conversion to a T 8N

53

Looking along the underside at the exhaust nozzles of the T 4

A well used ADEN gun pack on the underside of a T 4

The 'Welsh Wildcat' insignia of 233 OCU

**TECH PANEL**

Harrier GR 1

Scale: 1/48 Kit No: 05102

Price: £9.99

Type: Injection Moulded Plastic

Manufacturer: Airfix

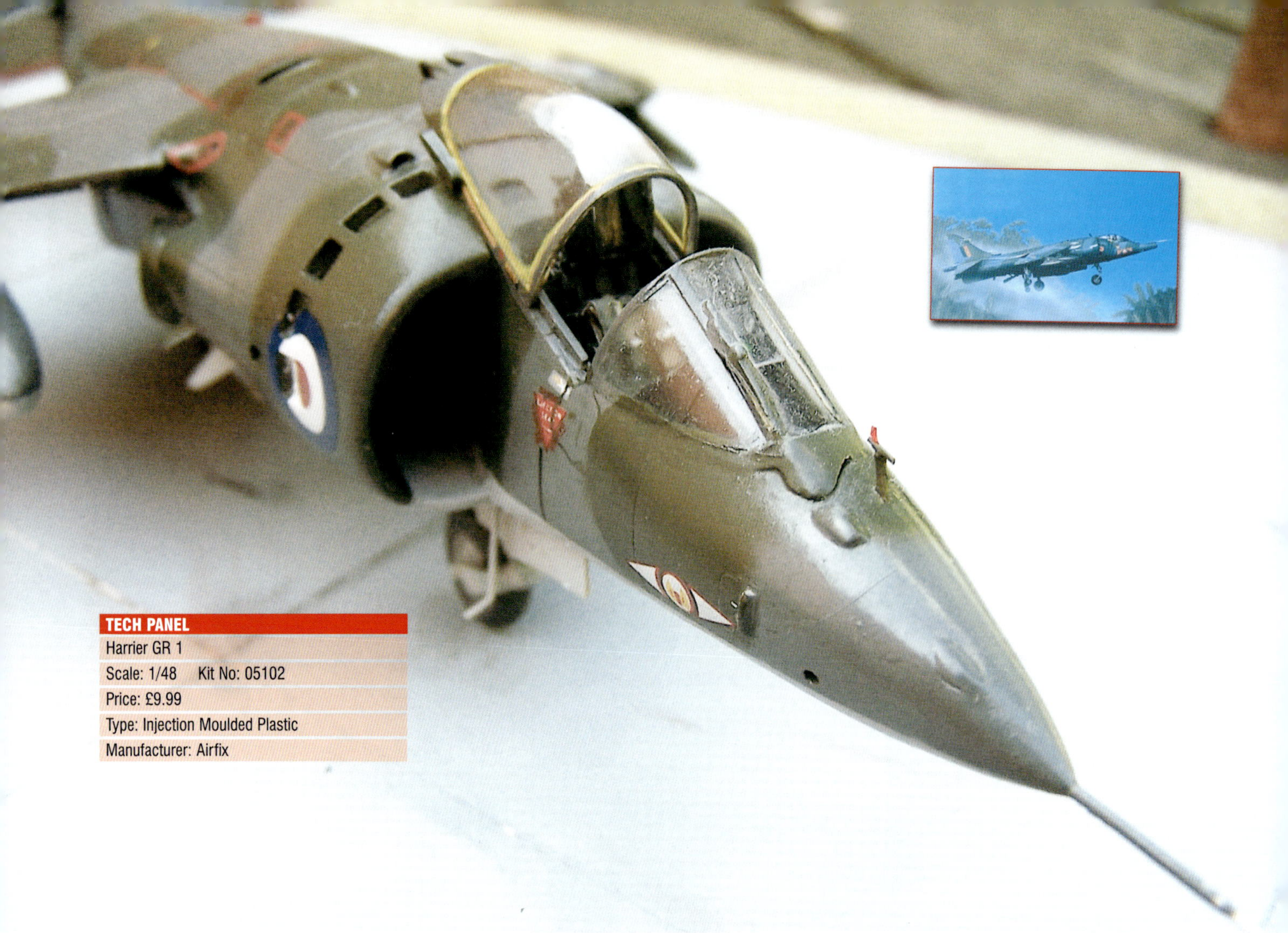

# A retrospective project

## Harrier GR 1 Conversion

By Bill Clark

I was totally mesmerised when I saw my first Harrier display – most likely at Biggin Hill around 1976. At that impressionable age I fell head-over-heels in love with the aircraft, and I just had to get my hands on a Harrier kit. I can vaguely remember trying to build various GR 1s in 1/72 from Airfix, Matchbox and then Hasegawa and a few years later attempting to convert them into the then new shape on the block, namely the GR 3.

There was an article in one of the modelling magazines of the day on how to convert Hasegawa's GR 1 into a GR 3 using balsa wood, dope and talcum powder and I tried, as best I could, to follow this article – mainly unsuccessfully. That particular Harrier conversion article must have been over thirty years ago. Times have indeed moved on, and during the passing of those three decades some new kits have emerged and I have managed to build up a nice little collection of 1/72 Harriers and Sea Harriers. More recently I've attempted to do something similar in 1/48, and so here I am trying to re-enact another early modelling event in my life, more or less in reverse, and in slightly larger scale!

The main problem is that first generation 1/48 Harrier kits aren't as good as any of the second generation Harriers available in that scale.

### Airfix's Harriers

Airfix entered the 1/48 V/STOL world quite late in the day, in fact their first foray was the Sea Harrier FRS 1 around 1983, and this kit, while dimensionally okay, lacked detail even for the early 1980s. This tool was used by Airfix for the basis of the Harrier GR 3 a couple of years later, using most of the original sprues but with a new fuselage, and it's this kit that I used on my back-dating exercise.

This particular model started off as a participant in an on-line Cold War Group build, and I wanted to depict one of the first Harriers

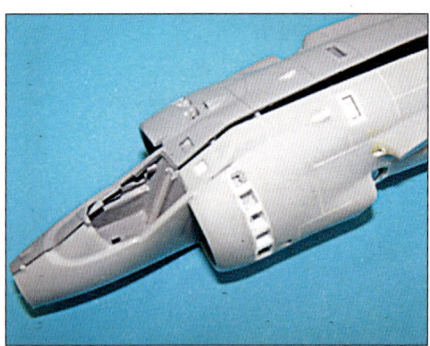

Upper fuselage detail. Few Harrier kits have depicted the intake doors correctly in any scale

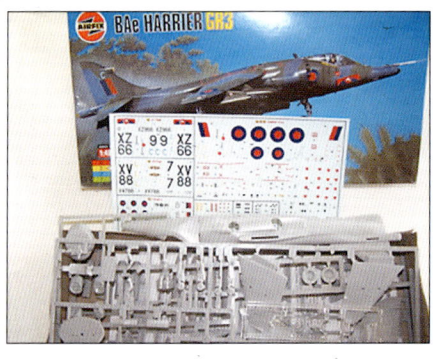

Airfix's GR.3 is lacking detail in some areas, but is as good a basis for starting as any

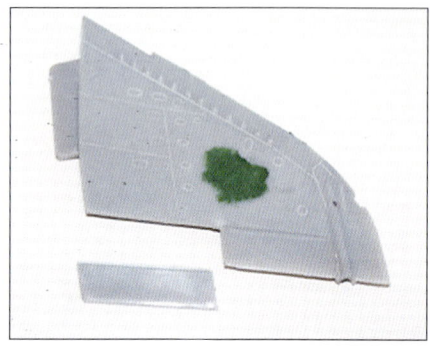

Newly scribed panels in the wing, and some corrections

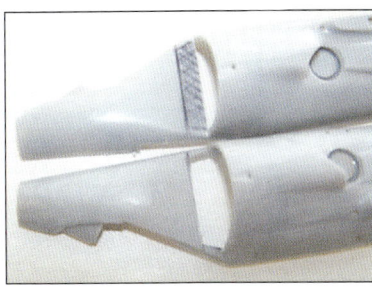

Hatched area to be removed from the inner intake area

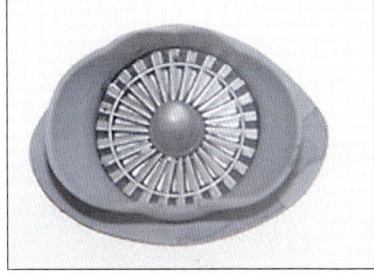

Engine compressor blades have been improved and detailed

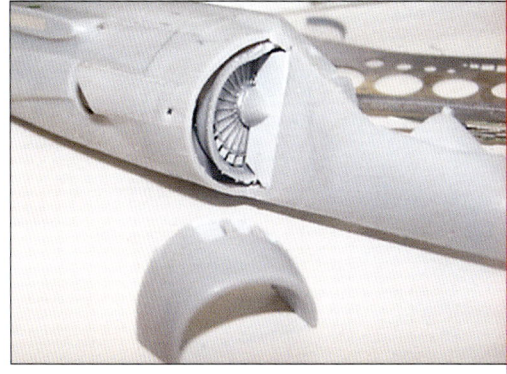

Plastic card and a section of Sea Eagle missile replacing removed plastic section

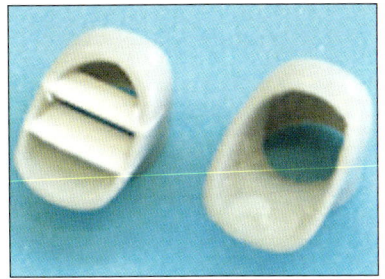

Forward Nozzles being attended to

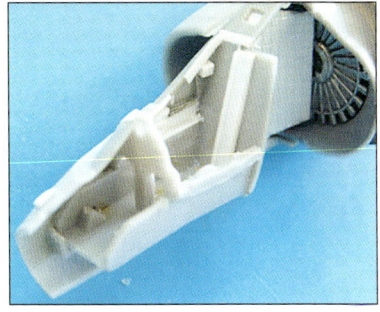

Cockpit tub with some additional detail added

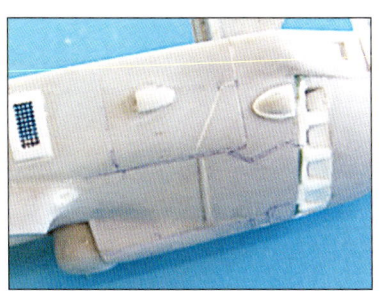

Further detail added to the upper fuselage

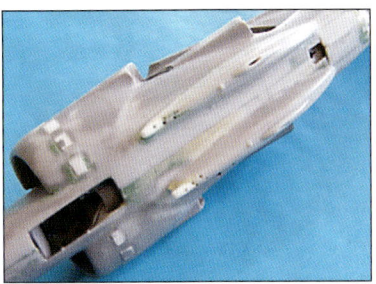

Aden cannon added – considerable additional detail was required

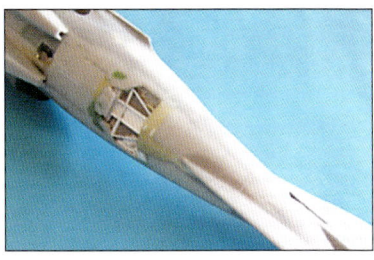

Rear fuselage showing additional air brake detailing

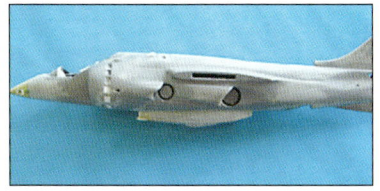

The completed fuselage with the new nose giving the correct profile

55

in service with No 1 Sqn. at RAF Wittering in the early very shiny 1969 delivery scheme. I missed the deadline by a long, long way. Good news is that the model is now ready for the 40th anniversary of the type's delivery next year.

What advantages does the Airfix kit have? The decals are very usable, and the kit is generally accurate in outline. The major negative point is the lack of detail throughout the kit. There are some aftermarket parts available, mainly from Heritage, but I decided to use as little as I could get away with, and in the end the only aftermarket add-on I ended up using was an Aeroclub Ejection Seat.

Before commencing this build/conversion I decided to list the areas for improvement. These included scribing in panel lines, opening the auxiliary air intakes, detailing and correcting the intake bells, opening up the solid exhaust nozzles, adding some detail to the airbrake well, extending the too small airbrake, detailing the outriggers, reprofiling the wing top vortex generators, replacing the wing fences and adding some detail to the rather sparse cockpit area . Most of this work is relevant to modellers building any Airfix Harrier in 1/48.

## Construction

As far as I am aware there is no aftermarket resin cockpit tub replacement for the Harrier in 1/48, so I used what I could from the kit and added plastic card and fusewire details. My initial plan was to use a resin seat from the NeoMega range, but this found its way into a Harrier GR 3 build, so I used an Aeroclub white metal item instead. I also opened up the two doors aft of the pilot on the rear decking, and added a HUD of sorts with additional plastic card detailing.

At this stage I also detailed and reprofiled the inner walls of the intake area. This involved removing a few millimetres of the kit's walls and replacing them with Plasticard to eventually form a 'V' shape in front of the compressor fan.

I decided to do as much work as possible on the fuselage first, so I removed the LRMTS (Lazer Ranged Marker Target Seeker) 'dolphin' nose from the kit as well as the FWR fairing on the fin. I rescribed various panel lines using a needle held in a pin vice using Dymo tape as a guide. I removed the front undercarriage doors and put as much detail in the resultant open gear bay as I could fit in.

The fuselage halves were joined and I removed some plastic 'W' shaped holes to portray the trough area below the tailplanes. It was then time to fashion the new pointy nose. I used a small piece of drop tank to form the core of this, adding a small boxed plastic card section where the oblique camera would go, along with a pitot tube of aluminium rod and needle. This was then encased in Milliput, and when dry sanded to shape. Various lumps and bumps were subsequently added.

Airfix's airbrake bay is a simple hole, so I added some internal detail. This bay is identical – certainly from what I could tell in modelling terms - on the GR 1, the SHAR and the GR 3, but the SHAR's airbrake – and that included in the kit - is too small for a GR 1 or GR 3, so needed a bit of extending. I added a small curved section of plastic card and faired this in. A pair of side strakes were also added. It's worth noting that the actual airbrake fitted flush over the fuselage skin on the real aircraft when closed.

I could have used replacement intakes, but decided to use the kit parts, as the work involved wouldn't be that difficult. The upper auxiliary intake doors were drilled out and replaced with plastic card walls and doors. Indentations for the lower doors were covered in plastic card to represent them in the closed position.

The new pointy nose in position

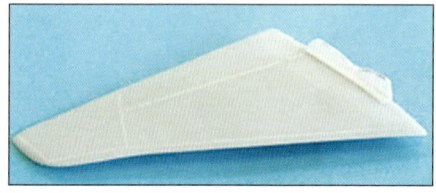

Tailplane with added scuff/strengthening plates

Wings added, and major construction complete

Test fitting the canopy parts

Reworked and super-detailed outriggers

Camouflage pattern in place on upper surfaces

The amended intakes were added and I tackled the Aden cannon next. These are very basic so new muzzles were added using plastic tube, and vents and blast holes added. The rear nozzle heat shields, depicted by Airfix as solid moulded blobs on the fuselage, had already been removed and backed with Milliput. New shields were borrowed from the Hasegawa GR 7 also being worked on, and these would be replaced in turn on that kit with photo-etched parts.

## It was then on to the wings…

I decided to rescribe as many of the panel lines as possible, and managed to overdo it a bit on one wing. The vortex generators are very poorly represented. I had used brass replacements by Airwaves and Flightpath on previous Harrier models but decided to use what I had on this kit. Rather than attempting to replace them all I tried a trick used by other Harrier SIG members in filing down the outer surfaces on the vertical, leaving a small sliver on the horizontal, to attempt to replicate the 'L' shaped prototypes.

The puffer jet nozzles were opened up. I also drooped the inner ailerons and added the fuel dump pipes with small sections from a very thin brass pin. The kit's wing fences are poorly shaped and didn't align very well, so these were removed. Slots were cut into the wing leading edge and sections of plastic card added. These were reprofiled when the glue had set.

Airfix's outriggers are very solid and had to be opened up with a drill and fine file. The rear actuator arms were made from aluminium tubing and rod. If you can't be bothered doing this then Aeroclub do replacements in white metal.

Undercarriage units and the front doors were added after a bit of detailing. Airfix's undercarriage units aren't that bad actually, though the wheel hubs are a bit bland. The lack of detail in this kit is highlighted chiefly by the very poor representation of the nozzles. All four were drilled hollow – not that easy a task – and new vanes were added from Plasticard let into horizontal slots in the nozzles' facings.

I originally wanted to feature my aircraft with a full complement of Matra SNEB pods, however the pods supplied in the kit are not accurate for this period or model. They depict those slightly larger with three rows of projectiles, used by the Royal Navy, and on GR 3s modified for the Falklands. I could have used those provided by Flightpath but eventually opted for a pair of 100 gallon drop tanks and empty outer pylons.

## Painting & Decorating

My GR 1 was now ready for the paint shop. A few coats of Halfords Grey primer had been added at various stages, and corrections attended to.

I used Xtracrylix for the main colours (their RAF colours are spot on). The Dark Sea Grey was applied first followed by the Dark Green using thin pieces of Blu-Tack as a mask to get a slightly feathered edge. Light Aircraft Grey was added to the lower surfaces using Tamiya masking tape for the hard demarcation line. Di-electric panels were depicted by painting these areas with a Tamiya Olive Drab mixture.

My GR 1 was going to be as glossy as I could get it, so numerous coats of Johnsons Klear were used to build up a nice hard finish. Decals were from the kit and various Modeldecal generic sheets.

I had a bit of a problem with the intake roundels as these appear over three of the auxiliary doors, and the upper two doors droop open when the aircraft is parked. I just about managed to get these to look okay by using a very sharp scalpel blade and quite a bit of Micro Sol and Micro Set. I gave the model a coat or two of Xtracylic gloss varnish to finish it off.

On the real GR 1 and GR 3 canopy a section on each side

of the frame is integral to the upper decking of the intakes. I added small sections of plastic card to the side of the canopy and these were very carefully sanded to shape. The clear sealant was applied by a thin wash of yellow paint. I had hoped to add the very prominent Miniature Detonating Cord in the clear canopy but never got around to that – I thought about using the decal supplied in the Hasegawa GR 7 though I'm not sure how accurate this would have been.

## Conclusion

This project took far too long to complete, but I'm glad I persevered – it's a nice shiny Harrier that shows how things were in those far flung days, and putting into perspective how far flung those days were, the Harrier entered RAF service the year after the last steam trains ran on British Rail, the Beatles were still together, and man set foot on the moon.

I'd like to think that I'll continue to add to my 1/48 Harrier collection, and in fact I already have a GR 7 and a GR 5 started using the Hasegawa kits, but how long they'll take to finish is another matter. With regard to the Airfix kit though, this could well form the basis of a future Kestrel FGA 1 project as well as a T 2 or T 4. We shall see!

# Chapter 6

# Sea Vixen

by Jack Trent
Pictures by Colin Pickett

Originally designed with both RAF and Navy in mind, the Sea Vixen was de Havilland's response to an Admiralty requirement for a Sea Venom replacement. Passed over by the RAF in favour of the Gloster Javelin, the D.H. 110, as it was initially known, earned immediate infamy following a disastrous incident at Farnborough Airshow in September 1952 when thirty-one people were killed after the aircraft broke up and one engine hit a spectator's area at the end of the runway.

It was not until 1955 that a navalised version of the prototype was demonstrated, and the following year the first arrested deck landing was made on *HMS Ark Royal*. The first Sea Vixen, the FAW 20, followed in 1957 and this was subsequently redesignated as the more familiar FAW 1 (Fighter-All-Weather). Over 100 aircraft entered service with the

Fleet Air Arm, with deliveries commencing in mid 1959.

The FAW 2 was an improved upgrade of the FAW 1 and in addition to the Firestreak was able to carry the Red Top AAM, four SNEB rocket pods and the air-to-ground Bullpup missile. An enlarged tail boom allowed for additional fuel tanks, in the extensions forward of the wing leading edge, and there was an improved escape system and room for additional electronic counter-measures equipment. The FAW 2 first flew in 1962 with twenty-nine new construction, and sixty-seven upgrades from FAW 1 entering service from 1964.

Destined to become the first British aircraft to operate without guns in the fighter/interceptor role, the FAW 1 was armed with four Firestreak air-to-air missiles, two Microcell unguided 2-inch (51 mm) rocket packs and could carry up to four 500 lb (230 kg) or two 1,000 lb bombs – although these latter could not be carried by the FAW 2. It was powered by two 50.0 kN (11,230 lbf) thrust Rolls-Royce Avon 208 turbojet engines, had a speed of 690 mph and a range of 600 miles.

Although it never became embroiled in any actual 'declared' wars, the operational career of the Sea Vixen saw a number of cruises on fleet carriers flying the flag in troubled waters. In 1964 Sea Vixens operated in the Persian Gulf, supporting British forces fighting against rebellious tribesmen in the Radfan, an action that saw the launch of air-strikes against the rebels. Sea Vixens helped cover the British withdrawal from Aden, and the aircraft had a presence over the Fleet in the background of several operations throughout the sixties as the sun set on the remains of the Empire. The FAW 1 was phased out of service from 1966 and the FAW 2 by 1972, replaced in the fixed wing role by F-4 Phantoms.

A handful of aircraft were subsequently converted for use as drones, and designated D 3. The uprated engine and removal of non-essential equipment allowed the D 3 to achieve true supersonic flight, but little use was ever made of the few aircraft converted. Some surplus machines also became target tugs, and were redesignated as TT.2s.

The bizarre 'cock-eyed' layout of the crew positions gave the aircraft something of the look of an airborne halibut according to some critics, and certainly the hole into which the observer was obliged to descend was regarded by many as a triumph of expediency over comfort. This aside, the swept wings and twin-boom configuration made the Sea Vixen unique among naval aircraft of its day, and nothing quite like it has flown off a carrier deck since.

This, then, was the comparatively simple career of the Sea Vixen. The aircraft flew in two naval display teams, and many airshow attendees will recall the last airworthy survivor, G-CVIX, in its gaudy

Red Bull livery. Thankfully repainted, this unlikely departure can only make one wonder how sweet the machine would have looked in the pale pearly greys of current US Navy aircraft. Now there is a 'what if' worth pursuing!

# The AirVix Classic

## Airfix's long-awaited new-tool Sea Vixen

By Tim Skeet

For years there were rumours that a mould existed at the back of an office somewhere for a larger scale Sea Vixen. Whatever the origin of this rumour, Airfix have now produced a model of this aircraft in 1/48 and managed to have it ready not only for the Christmas season, but also, coincidentally, at a point when the Navy has once more lost its fixed wing fighters in the recent defence review.

The Sea Vixen is a very British 'special interest' machine, produced in limited numbers, serving only in the Royal Navy, seeing no notable combat service, and having a fairly short service career. The type is, however, notable as being the last de Havilland fighter, and the first missile armed fully all-weather Naval interceptor. Moreover, one of these machines is still flying, thirty years after the type left front line service.

Designed in the 1950s, flown operationally through the late 1950s and 1960s, retired in the early 1970s, the Sea Vixen first entered service as the FAW 1 before being replaced by the FAW 2, the subject of this kit. In 1/72 both versions are available from various manufacturers, and now at last, we have an injection moulded Sea Vixen in the larger scale. As a modeller, I have long admired the Vixen

1:48 DE HAVILLAND SEA VIXEN FAW.2
TECH PANEL

| | |
|---|---|
| Scale: 1/48 | |
| Kit No: 11001 | |
| Type: Injection Moulded Plastic | |
| Manufacturer: Airfix | |

and built several of the old Frog kits. Over the past dozen years I have also been assisting in small ways with the preservation of XP924, the last flying example, which will soon be celebrating ten years from the date it received its Permit to Fly in March 2001. Note also that 2011 marks another anniversary for the Sea Vixen, this being the 60th anniversary of the first flight of the prototype D.H.110, which took place in September 1951.

First impressions of the new Airfix kit are good. Having built the other 1/48 Sea Vixen kit, the Dynavector vacform model, I was really looking forward to this one, and it had all the appearance of a

The kit builds up in a number of sub-components. The cockpit area comes as a box that slots in from below the upper fuselage half, but the horizontal split along the fuselage needs a little filler to get right. Don't forget plenty of weight in the nose, particularly if the wings are modelled up as their angle transfers the centre of gravity

The intake ducting and tailpipes pre-fitted into the lower fuselage half. These parts are well engineered and a good fit

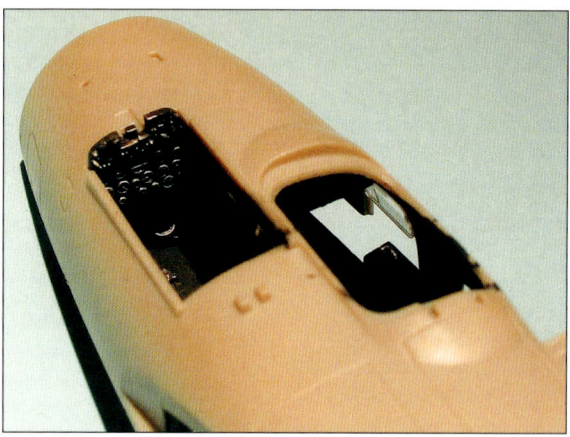

The kit instrument panel is not at all bad and looks good with simple dry brushing

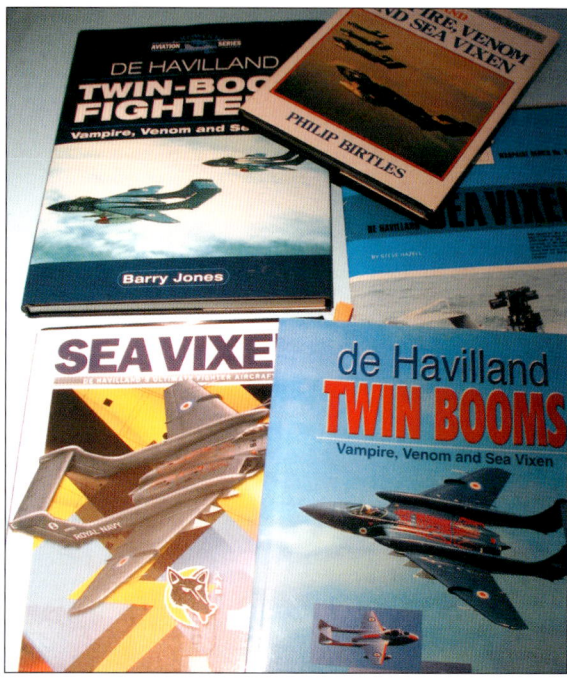

There are lots of good reference works available on the Sea Vixen, including some good shots of '924

straightforward build. The instructions are exemplary, well laid out, clear, and idiot proof, and with options for different flap, airbrake, undercarriage, tail hook, wing and canopy positions, there are a number of choices to make. With all the control surfaces as separate features, besides the expected wingfold option, the kit offers several interesting display possibilities. I intended modelling XP924, wings up, airbrake sagging, cockpit open and ready to go. The kit even include weighted and unweighted main wheels (though not

unweighted extended oleos), a nice touch. A purist might also want to modify the main undercarriage leg braces as these are not quite the right shape, but I have not done this on the model.

For anyone intending to model XP924 as seen in its most recent incarnations on the airshow circuit, there are a few detail points to note. The observer's cockpit 'lid' should be left clear, not painted black. The lid is made of clear Perspex, but in service was painted black to keep out the light and help the observer view his radarscope. On '924 the paint was scraped off to make the 'coal hole' less claustrophobic. Incidentally, the Vixen side window is also fitted with a roller blind (which '924 has lost). Furthermore, the in-flight refuelling probe should be left off with only a small stub fitted in its place. This appears to be supplied as part 90C, but is not referred to in the instructions.

Inside the observer's cabin, the radar console and equipment have been cleared out leaving a large empty space, although while the machine operated at Llanbedr as a D 3 this space was filled by the remote control gear- and there remains a mass of wiring and 'bits' down there, none of which I have attempted to model. Likewise, the nose does not have the radar scanner, only a large lump of lead ballast. '924 has not carried any stores while acting as a display machine, although is now cleared and equipped to carry drop tanks on the outer pylons, something which may happen if the machine appears at displays in 2011.

A rough coat of paint (Xtracolor XA1005 Extra Dark Sea Grey acrylic paint) to show up blemishes

A glossy white underside - kept clean as '924 is maintained in near spotless condition. Be careful with the airbrake position. Note the slightly drooping main inner doors. Two protuberances should also be added to the rear underside of the fuselage, which I attached at the very end of the build

I left the outer wing panels off until almost the end. This makes the job much easier

The observer's canopy hood is clear on '924. Internal handle detail has been added from scratch

The Airfix kit stands alongside the old 1/72 Frog kit. We have come a very long way in terms of kit technology! This also shows the attractive yellow and red scheme that XP924 carried at Llanbedr

The Red Top missiles and rocket pods in the kit, though nicely produced, will have to sit in the spares box. Note also that '924, while in its Llanbedr colours and later Red Bull livery, did not carry the outer pylons. The Llanbedr version (yellow and red colours) also had the small wing camera bulges above and below the wing tips. These were deleted when the aircraft was put into the Red Bull finish.

Although I was building the kit 'out of the box', the seats do need some harnesses. They are nicely depicted with top and bottom firing handles, but without the seat and parachute harness, they do not look the part. A pair of crew figures are included, so these can be used to mask this omission, but the seats will need more prominent rectangular headrests. The observer's seat is, however, the wrong shape - it differs from the pilot's seat as it is rounded at the shoulders, not square. Otherwise, the main cockpit and observer's 'coal hole' are nicely portrayed.

On '924, as currently configured, there is no gunsight - instead there is a cluster of radios fitted here that finish flush with the instrument panel. The internal colour is the usual charmless black, for which I used Revell Panzer Grey with a silver enamel paint dry brush and was pleased with the result. The kit provides most of the detail and it all fits together well.

The model is well thought out. There is an option to display the Vixen in approach mode on a stand, with everything extended, and

61

The Sea Vixen taxis out for a display at Kemble. Big, noisy and impressive

An overview of the main cockpit. The gunsight has been replaced by some additional radio equipment

non-flattened wheels. The tail hook has two positions, one for on the ground, the other at full extension for display on the stand (which will need to be ordered separately from Airfix). The airbrake likewise has a fully deployed position or a drooped look on the ground. Note that the airbrake can be cranked down on the ground for maintenance purposes, and will sag. However, it never properly opens when the undercarriage is down, so do not try to model the suggested configuration in the instructions.

The flaps have been equally well thought out with extra parts for the extended flaps option and good internal detail provided. Like many naval aircraft, the flaps are large and need to be effective. These are not extended when the wings are folded - although they can be manually cranked down for maintenance. With wings extended, the flaps may be left out. I have checked these details with Paul Kingsbury, XP924's Chief Engineer. The flaps on '924 are currently painted white on their internal surfaces, while the undercarriage and hook bays are described as being a pale white-grey with a green tinge.

Another area that has been well designed is the complex intake ducting. Some care needs to be taken with the seams, although not much can be seen once the whole kit has been built, but this is not an issue at all with the neat tail pipes, moulded as one-piece cylinders.

Other well executed details include the wingfold. Various parts are provided to form a strong attachment for the outer wing panels when extended, or alternatively detailed blanks and hinges are included for the folded option, and the wing stays, usually fitted when the aircraft is resting, are included. There is a small error of positioning here, as they attach to points on the wing upper surfaces some eight inches inboard of the fences, not on the fences as suggested in the

instructions. The stays are red in colour. As a final detail note on XP924 as she is currently configured parts 51C and 52C should not be used. There are also three underwing whip aerials fitted.

The Sea Vixen has a complex shape, but the breakdown of parts has achieved a good balance between number of parts, fit and accuracy. I found that a little filler was inevitably needed along the horizontal fuselage join, and a little on the pylon joints, but not much elsewhere. I have to praise Airfix for the fit of the parts, making this model a real pleasure to build. Moreover, the level of detail is such that there is no real need to add anything, although naturally this will not stop the detail specialists or after-market firms.

The kit offers four FAW 2 operational schemes, all in Extra Dark Sea Grey over White. There are other colourful alternatives available from Model Alliance, whose sheet ML48197 offers several colourful trials and target schemes, including one of '924's sister ships at Llanbedr, which had a different red/yellow scheme from '924.

Once built straight from the box, this kit is impressive. With wings folded it does not take up so much horizontal space - just watch out for height. This is a large model. With all the various options and potential colours Airfix have given the enthusiast a high quality basis from which to model a colourful and smart range of these 1960s fighters. I will certainly look forward to buying a few more examples of this kit.

# Fox One – Fox from the Box

### Xtrakit's Sea Vixen as it comes

By Bernie Montague

**M**odelling the Sea Vixen has always been a challenge with the somewhat dated and inaccurate FROG kit and its reissues, so it was with great excitement that the news of a brand new Sea Vixen Kit was received earlier this year.

The box-top has an eye-catching painting of XP924 in its D 3 guise. Inside are four medium grey sprues and one clear, all separately bagged, containing 73 grey and 6 clear parts. A small bag of resin goodies is included too, consisting of some nice little air intakes and catapult strop horns for the lower fuselage, nose, undercarriage and doors, as well as two strangely under-scale seats. All the mouldings are crisp with some great panel detail – although the moulding ejector posts are somewhat heavy and the wing trailing edges are quite thick. Certainly what comes in the box promises to build into a great representation of the Sea Vixen FAW 2 and there are all the parts you would need to make up an FAW 1 if so desired.

## Construction

Construction started with the cockpit, which consists of eleven parts including two ejection seats in resin. These look undersized, so I used an Aeroclub Mk 4 seat for the pilot and the kit part for the Navigator, as it would not be as noticeable with the canopy closed. One

| TECH PANEL | |
|---|---|
| Scale: 1/72 | |
| Kit No: 72003 | |
| Type: Injection Moulded Plastic | |
| Manufacturer: Xtrakit | |

inaccuracy I have found with the cockpit is that the joystick location is too far aft and so should be relocated 1.5 mm forward of the marked location. This will allow the pilot's seat to locate properly.

The pilot's and navigator's consoles were sprayed Tamiya Nato Black, as was the completed cockpit tub, with dials picked out in black and glossed with Johnson's floor polish. The seats were painted with reference to pictures on the excellent Martin Baker website.

The internal components for the fuselage were tackled next, the first of these being the three-part intake duct and dummy engine faces. All three parts were sprayed with Tamiya silver (X11). When dry, the fan blades were given a wash of thinned acrylic black to bring out the detail but looked unconvincing, and I was starting to think about intake blanking plates at this time - something I try not to use. The fan blade bulkhead was attached and the completed assembly

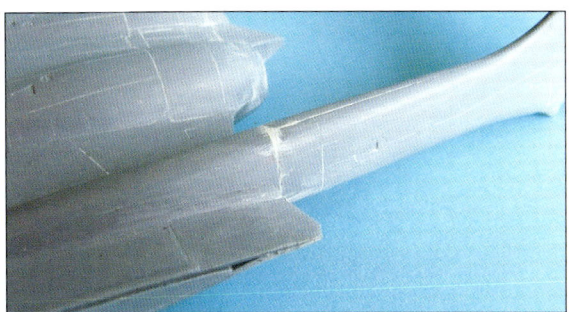

The booms, nose and exhaust fairing were all faired in with more filler and sanded after setting

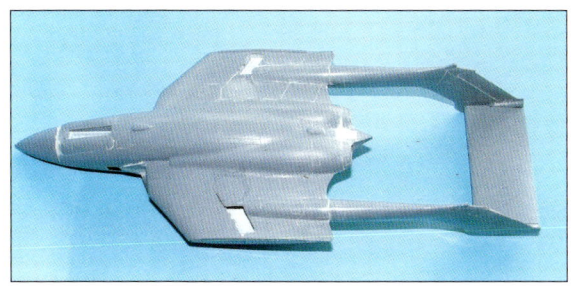

The almost completed underside – note the filled-in arrestor hook fairing

63

The balsa plugs designed to strengthen the tail boom joint were both strong and light – an advantage with a potential tail-sitter

offered up to the bottom fuselage half, achieving a perfect fit.

Before I went any further I checked the fit of top and bottom fuselage halves. As there are no locating pips, alignment is a bit iffy and I then noticed the rather thick trailing edges. Concerned that this would affect the fit of the booms I taped these together and offered them up to the relevant positions. The upshot was that I could get away with thinning the trailing edges and this would allow a smooth transition between wings and booms.

Main and nose-wheel bays were now cemented in place. Before you fix the intake assembly remove the web that stretches between the intake fronts as this prevents the cockpit tub from locating

The wing blanking plates are handed, so were marked carefully while still on the sprue to avoid confusion

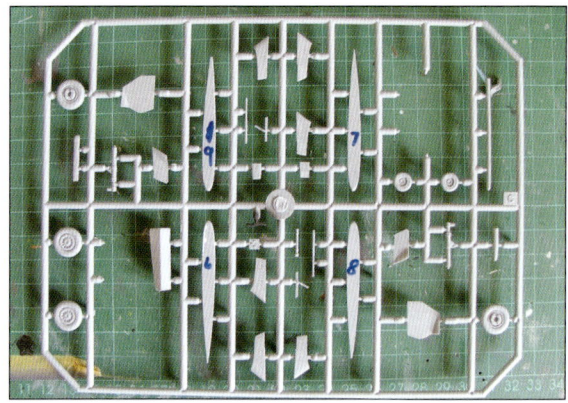

properly. After cementing the fuselage halves I noticed large gaps around the areas where the intakes were supposed to join to the fuselage. My mind was then made up: intake blanking plates. Problem solved. Another problem here is the shape and position of the navigator's window, which is also 2mm too low. The lower edge of the window has square corners, whilst the uppers are rounded, so I applied a bit of filler to the lower edges of the window corners and rounded them with a needle file when set.

The booms are a butt fit to the trailing edges. If you are building the FAW 2 version it is not so much of an issue as the pinion tanks will provide additional support, but some form of assistance will definitely be needed for earlier versions. I decided to err on the side of caution and carved some internal supports from balsa. I fitted the booms using some slow-setting super-glue. This was followed by the

A close-up of the front end showing the finished blanking plates in position

tailplane, nose-cone (with 20 grams of lead weight) and exhaust fairing. Be careful with the exhaust pipes as there is not a lot of gluing area – I cemented mine one at a time allowing the cement to set fully before inserting the other. Incidentally, there should only be about ½ mm protruding from the fairing.

The booms, nose and exhaust fairing were all faired in with more filler and sanded after setting. I had most difficulty with the over-wing fairings (pinion tanks), and a quick test-fit showed that the fitting of these parts was not going to be easy. On the full size machine, these sit flush on the tops of the booms, so it was out with the trusty No 10 blade for more scraping, followed by some harsh sanding to get them to fit.

It was at this time that I fitted the wing blanking plates. These are a great idea as they will enable you to assemble the model with the wings folded, albeit with a lot of scratch-building. Due to the fact that I had removed quite a bit of material from the trailing edges, I had to shorten the inserts by about 10mm to get them to fit. Outer wing panels were butt-jointed to the fuselage section, as the blanking plates provided a large gluing area.

## Painting

After priming the model was sprayed overall with Xtracrylix RAF Rescue Yellow (XA1019), which was supplied (along with RAF Red Arrows Red) with the review kit. I changed over to using acrylics about three years ago, trying out various manufacturers and now use them exclusively for finishing all of my models. I picked up some Xtracrylix paints at the Scottish Nationals at Perth last year and was totally won over by them. Some people have problems airbrushing acrylics, but if you turn down the pressure on your compressor (15-20psi) and use cleaner regularly, then all will be fine.

The Yellow was thinned 40% with Tamiya thinner and applied in several light coats to build an even overall smooth finish. After allowing to harden for a day, I applied the supplied masks for the

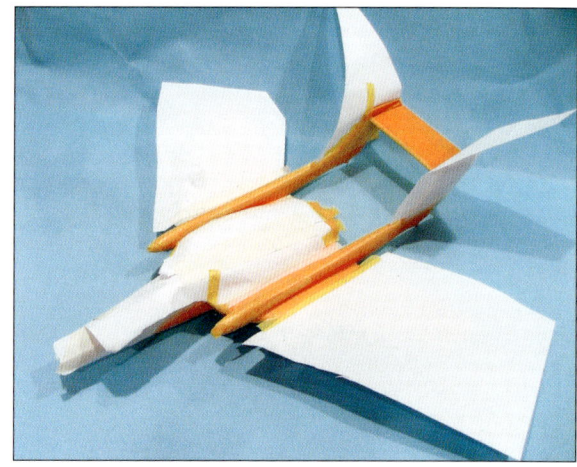

Masking was completed with Tamiya Tape and paper

Micro Set under the decals helped to bed them down nicely into the recessed detail

tricky curves around the nose and tail-booms and these went on with no problems. Masking was completed with Tamiya tape and paper and then I airbrushed with the Red.

Decals were applied straight onto the surface of the paint without any gloss coat, the finish is that good! The model was sprayed after decalling with a mix of Xtracrylix Flat Varnish and Johnson's Klear, thinned with Tamiya Thinners. The result was a smooth satin finish, which I find appropriate in this scale, and this caused any decal carrier film to disappear completely. A dark grey wash was applied to selective panel lines as I didn't want to overdo the effect.

## Finishing Touches

The painting instructions call for the pylons to be finished in Yellow, but the photos that I have of XP294 show these to be Red. Pitot tubes were finished in silver with yellow bases. Photos show a prominent blade aerial under the nose just forward of the nosewheel door but none is provided with the kit, so I used a piece of 10 thou Plasticard suitably shaped for this. Two whip aerials behind the cockpit were made from fine fuse wire, painted white and fixed in position with white glue. Wingtip and nosewheel door navigation lights were painted in silver and overcoated with Tamiya Clear Red and Green.

Masking was then removed from the transparencies and that was it!

Would I build another one? Absolutely! When compared to the old Frog/Revell offering, the glaring inaccuracies of the old kit stand out. I have another one on order and can't wait to finish it as a FAW 1 using all the extra new resin goodies from FAA Models.

# Fox Two

## Upgrading The Xtrakit Sea Vixen

By Steve Muntus

I clearly remember the first time I ever saw a Sea Vixen. I was visiting the Fraser Gunnery range near Portsmouth as a young Sea Cadet. A constant steam of Sea Vixens was flying overhead with their distinctive twin-boom tails flashing in the afternoon Sun. This started my life-long love affair with de Havilland's most striking fighter and kindled an interest in Fleet Air Arm aircraft, so naturally, when The Ark Royal Project was asked to build two versions of the new Xtrakit model of the Sea Vixen, Bernie Montague and I were delighted to take up the challenge.

## Upgrading the Kit

Like many limited run injection kits the Sea Vixen has all the right basics but is a blank canvas for refinements and additions. There is plenty of scope to include some of the typical features of a naval aircraft, such as a folding nose or wings or a complete arrester hook

assembly that can be posed in the open position. Another area crying out for action is the prominent airbrake on the lower fuselage, which is only represented by panel lines and two resin guide vanes.

The nice two-part intake ducts look great but the Rolls Royce Avon Mk 108 engine faces are only very basic and inaccurate representations. None-the-less the kit has great engraving and panel

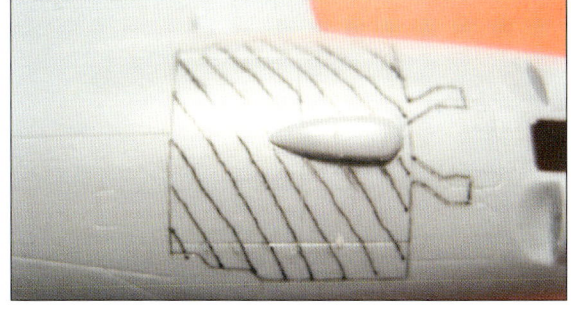

**Panel lines were carefully marked out and apertures opened for the airbrake and arrestor hook**

65

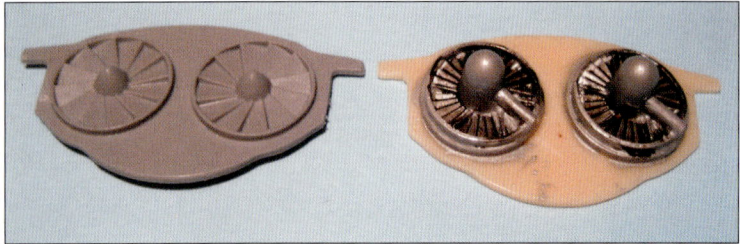

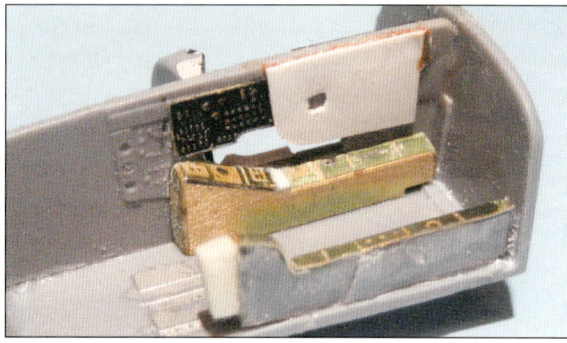

Cockpit detail underway. The central dividing wall is not solid in the real aircraft, so a suitably shaped hole was cut in it and more etched brass detail added

The fan detail on the kit is poor, so a more accurate representation, including the prominent air starter duct, was scratchbuilt and cloned in resin to produce two new ones, which were then reset in the back plate

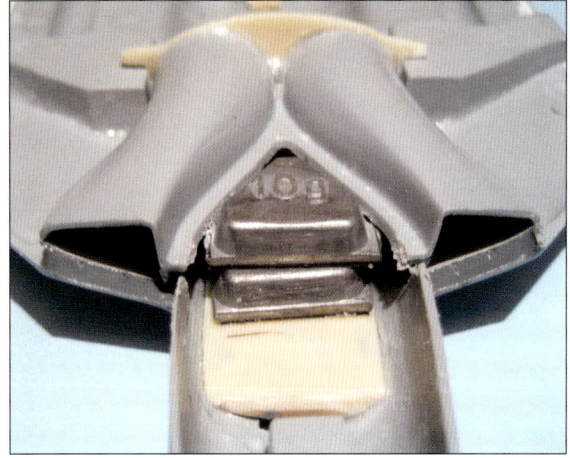

Don't forget to put in plenty of weight in the front end to avoid an almost certain tail-sitter. To allow for the open nose radar bay, and given the extra weight of the resin upgrade parts, suitable weight was added between the intake assemblies

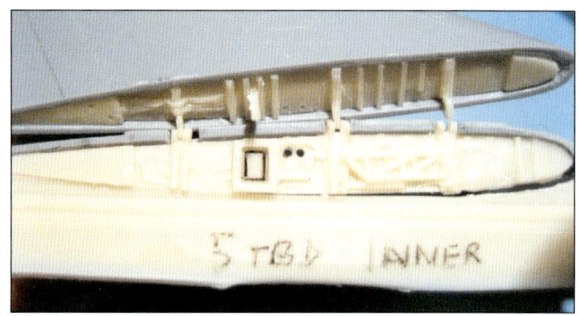

The supporting ridges for the kit supplied blanking plates (Parts C6 and C7) were scraped away and new ridges added 1mm further inboard

detail and is full of promise. With my penchant for creating resin upgrade sets, I couldn't wait to set about making up some masters for resin parts that I could use to build a more detailed representation of my favourite aircraft.

## Construction begins

Starting with the lower fuselage I carefully located the panel lines as moulded and opened up the airbrake and arrester hook apertures in readiness for fitting my resin interior detail parts. At this stage all moulding towers on both upper and lower fuselages were removed and the rear edges of the inner wing panels were carefully thinned down to allow a sharper trailing edge and a closer fit for the tail booms when fitted. Once the airbrake and arrester hook housings had been superglued in place my attention turned to the cockpit area.

As no pilot's instrument panel coaming is provided I made one up using Plasticard and Milliput and attached it to the upper fuselage. Brass detail from the Airwaves Sea Vixen Interior detail set was modified to replace the original instrument panel and side consoles, and the pilot's instrument panel was attached to the new coaming so as to align with the rear of the front canopy fairing.

On the observer's side the radar panel was moved aft to match up with the vertical dividing line in the small side window (so that's

All the elements of the jet pipe assembly were combined and the arrestor hook recess was reshaped. Once complete, a one-piece resin copy was made which again served to align everything at the rear of the fuselage

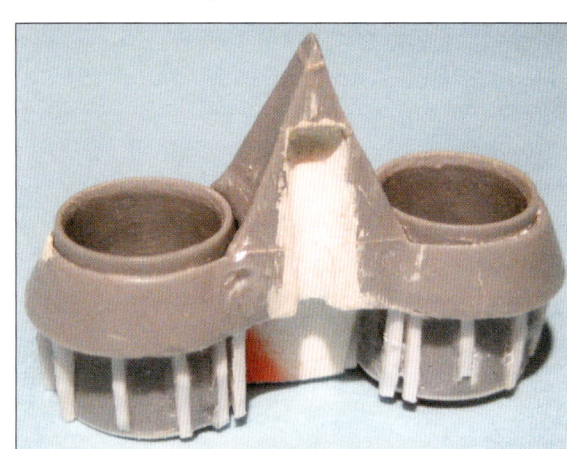

what it's for)! The floor at the rear of the observer's 'Coal Hole' was also cut out and replaced with thinner Plasticard set about 2 mm lower than the original, so as to allow a correctly scaled seat to fit in without poking out of the access hatch. As with most fighters of the period the preferred finish is black on black so a coat of Tamiya Nato Black was followed by grey and white dry brushing to bring out the detail. Having noted that the observer's window was set too low on the starboard fuselage, (so as to match up with the horizontal join line) I moved it up by 1.5mm and added a new sill from scrap plastic.

The real aircraft's full air intakes have clearly visible seam lines so I scribed these into the inside surfaces of the upper and lower halves before joining them. I addressed the poor fan face detail by drilling them out of their back plate. A more accurate representation, including the prominent air starter duct, was scratchbuilt and cloned in resin to produce two new ones and the complete assembly fitted to the lower fuselage.

Before fitting the main undercarriage bays, their inner doors were fitted in their closed position. I also needed to make room for my resin wing fold inserts so the supporting ridges for the kit-supplied blanking plates (parts C6 and C7) were scraped away and new ridges added 1mm further inboard to accommodate the wingfold hinge points. I cut out the corresponding slots in the upper fuselage.

A notable problem with this kit is the lack of any support for the butt joints between the tail booms and the main fuselage, and the tail pipe assembly which just sits on the rear of the fuselage. The boom issue was solved as seen when Bernie Montague whipped up a couple of balsa plugs (from which I made resin copies) and the latter helped strengthen and align the tail booms nicely. As the jet pipe assembly is quite complex, I combined all the elements except the kit-provided resin 'Plugs' and took the opportunity to correct the shape of the arrester hook recess underneath as well as making space for the scratchbuilt internal part of the housing. Once complete, a one-piece resin copy was made which again served to align everything at the rear of the fuselage.

After much careful test fitting and adjustment the fuselage halves were finally mated in such a way to allow my scratchbuilt wing fold inserts to slot into place once all the joints had set thoroughly.

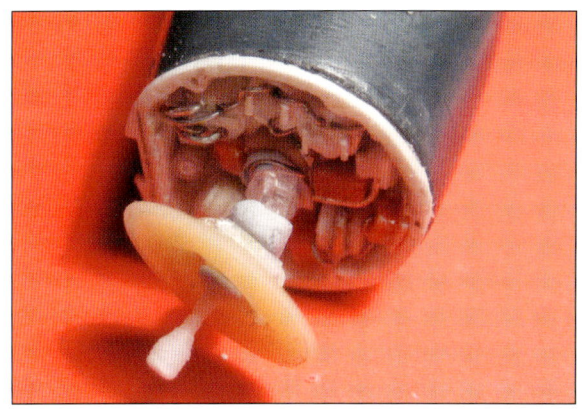

In anticipation of Xtrakit's release a scratchbuilt radar bay assembly had already been prepared using an old Frog Sea Vixen as a template

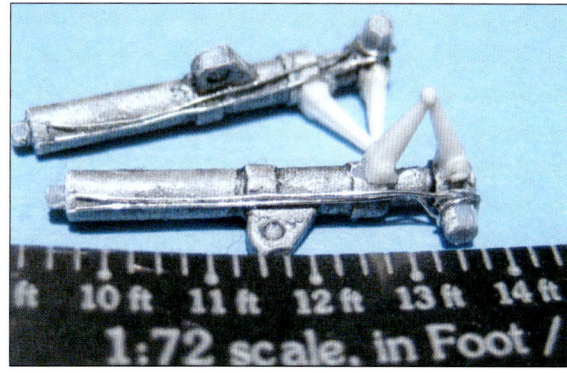

Although a delicate resin nose undercarriage leg and wheel are provided, the main undercarriage legs are very basic so some brake pipes from fuse wire and a pair of scissor jacks were added from the spares box

The intake splitter plates are moulded integrally with the upper and lower fuselage halves, and this means that the resulting horizontal split would be very hard to clean up. It also became apparent that despite there being a full intake trunking the joint line between this and the splitter plates was fairly ungainly looking, so I decided to make up one-piece replacement splitter plates which would avoid having to clean up a horizontal joint line and also overlap the intake trunking joint and add the missing bleed air duct as a bonus. Just in front of the apex of each splitter plate I added a small triangular fairing.

In anticipation of Xtrakit's release I had already scratchbuilt a radar bay assembly using an old Frog Sea Vixen as a template. This was quickly updated to fit the Xtrakit and once the square hinge area on the right side of the nose had been cut out, the resin radar bay was plugged into the forward fuselage and fared in with Greenstuff. A new nose cone with integral mating ring and hinge was also made up, cloned and fitted at the end of the painting process.

Finally after a quick clean up and correction of any minor flaws, the model was ready to be painted.

## Colour Options

When I was first offered the chance to be involved in this twin kit build, I thought about completing the FAW 2 as XP924 in its typical 899 NAS markings. Unfortunately that aircraft never operated off *HMS Ark Royal*, so I decided to complete the model as an 893 NAS machine XN684, which worked from our favoured aircraft carrier during the 1970s.

One bonus in the kit which is not mentioned in the instructions is a superb set of masks for the transparencies. Once these had been fitted, the open cockpits masked off and the intakes and jet pipes packed with damp kitchen tissue, the whole aircraft was sprayed with Halford's acrylic white undercoat and allowed to dry for 24 hours before being sanded back with 6000 grade Micro-mesh. The distinctive colour scheme was then applied using Xtracrylix White for the under surfaces and – following extensive masking - Extra Dark Sea Grey from the same range for the upper surfaces. Flat Silver was used for all open access panels and undercarriage parts. I applied the markings for my chosen 893 NAS machine using the excellent XtraDecal Sea Vixen set 72077. Only then was the model subjected to a final coat of future making the carrier film virtually invisible.

As naval aircraft were always maintained in good order, only light weathering was applied to the airframe, with slightly heavier staining on the lower fuselage.

## Final Assembly

Once all the painting was finished, I added all the extra pieces, open nose and radar dish, airbrake, arrester hook and canopies. Unusually, I secured the outer undercarriage doors using Gator glue before the main undercarriage was attached! This helped when fitting the main

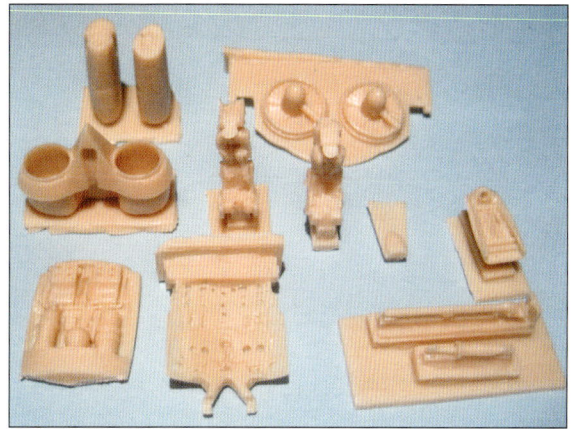

All the resin detail sets employed in this build are now available from FAA Models via A2Zee

undercarriage legs to give them slight forward rake and match up with the groove in each door.

The kit comes with two large drop tanks but no other underwing stores. I noticed that when in service a common practice was to use a converted Sea Hawk drop tank as a baggage carrier and this aircraft features a nice yellow squadron lightning flash on it as well. Looking through my spares box I found one and mounted it on the port inner faring.

## Conclusion

The upgraded Xtrakit Sea Vixen was certainly a challenge to build but with a little care it developed into a really nice example of the type. I would recommend it to anyone as a chance to gain experience in building limited run injection kits.

| TECH PANEL | |
|---|---|
| Scale: | 1/48 |
| Kit No: | 09180 |
| Status: | Reissue |
| Panel Lines: | Recessed |
| Type: | Injection Moulded Plastic |
| Parts: | Plastic 144, Clear 6 |
| Decal Options: | 5 |
| Manufacturer: | Airfix |

# Buccaneer

## Hawker Siddely Buccaneer S2, S2B, S2C, S2D, S50

By Mark Chadbourne

The Blackburn Buccaneer served with the Royal Navy and the Royal Air Force between 1962 and 1994, including service in the 1991 Gulf War. Designed and initially produced by Blackburn Aircraft at Brough, it was later known as the Hawker Siddeley Buccaneer when Blackburn became a part of the Hawker Siddeley group.

### Airfix's kit in 1/48

### The Kit

The large box contains seven sprues of light grey plastic and one clear. A lot of the parts had come away from the sprues and were rattling around in the bottom of the bag. You also get two instruction manuals, one for the S2B and another for the S2, S2C, S2D and S50, and two large decal sheets with options for six aircraft in five different colour schemes

### Construction

The cockpit is very sparse and utilises decals for the instrument panels. The seats are very good and could easily be made into fine representations of the Martin-Baker B Mk 6BSB-2. Prior to building this kit I had heard a lot of stories about fit of its parts, and in this instance horizontally-split fuselage halves were so warped that at the stub section of the wings had a two-centimetre gap. The only way to combat this is to join the halves a little bit at a time, making sure that the parts are held firmly in place at all times using tape, clamps, bulldog clips, and rubber bands. Once you have the fuselage halves together you then come to the intakes. Suffice to say the only way I got them to fit was to have them flush at the top and then use copious amounts of filler on the undersides.

If you manage to get this far with the build of your Buccaneer, take heart, because things get easier from now on. After filling and sanding of the fuselage is complete, the rest of the kit goes together without too much pain.

## Colour Options

There's something for everyone here: an S2C from *HMS Ark Royal* in 1970, an S2D again from *HMS Ark Royal* but from 1976, an S2 from *HMS Eagle* in 1966), a South African Air Force S50 based at Waterkloof in 1970, an S2B from Lossiemouth in 1988, and finally an S2B from *Operation Desert Storm* in 1991. I chose the S2 from *HMS Eagle* (simply because I was born in 1966!). The decals went on fine,

although I found them a little thick. I used no setting solutions and only a couple of the smaller items silvered

## Conclusion

The fit of the main parts is very bad and because of this I can't really recommend it to younger modellers. The more wrinkled modellers among us (yours truly included) could make a very good representation out of this kit. Many accessories are available and can only enhance it. Airfix are to be applauded for the amount of colour and decal options available out of the box, and I think it represents real value for money.

# Blackburn's Sky Pirate

## Waiting for a War

By Jack Trent

The catalogue of the Blackburn aircraft company makes interesting reading, chiefly for the long string of also-rans, not-quites, and never-wozzers produced over its long history. Contraptions like the Dart, the Blackburn and the Ripon were, in their way, moderately successful workaday types, and while the Skua scored some notable firsts, these were largely by default, and nowhere in the company's history do we find the stuff of legends – no Spitfire, no Hurricane, and no Swordfish. Until, that is, they came up with the Buccaneer.

Designed in the 1950s as a low-level strike aircraft with nuclear capabilities, the Buccaneer was initially a Naval machine, and was brought into being to tackle the threat of the Soviet Sverdlov class cruisers. The specification called for a two-seat aircraft with folding wings, capable of flying at Mach 0.85 at 200 ft (61 m), having a combat range of over 400 nautical miles, and carrying a nuclear weapon internally. Blackburn's design won the tender, offering several advanced features, including an area-ruled fuselage, variable incidence tailplane, and a rotating bomb bay, which overcame the

problem of opening doors at high speed in a low-level strike

As the small wing, designed for the low-level mission, was inappropriate for low-speed carrier operations, the tail cone was designed to open as an airbrake and this, coupled to the folding wings and nose, facilitated operations on the cramped decks and hangars of British aircraft carriers.

The underpowered S 1 could not get off the deck fully laden and was obliged to operate with a buddy system, sortieing with a Scimitar, which would deliver the full load of fuel by aerial refuelling. Matters were alleviated by the arrival of the S 2, fitted with the Rolls-Royce Spey turbofan, and this, with its enlarged engine nacelles and some wing modifications, had completely replaced the S 1 by November 1966.

The RAF adopted the Buccaneer in 1968, following the cancellation of both the TSR 2 and F-111K. Forty-six new aircraft were built by Blackburn's successor, Hawker Siddeley, designated S 2B. These had RAF-type communications and avionics equipment, Martel air-to-surface missile capability, and could be equipped with a bulged bomb-bay door containing an extra fuel tank. Some Navy Buccaneers were modified in-service to carry the Martel, and these were later redesignated S 2D.

No dual-control trainer versions of the Buccaneer were constructed, and the FAA and the RAF utilised the two-seat Hawker Hunter T 8B and T 7A respectively for Buccaneer conversion training. These Hunter variants had a modified instrument panel to simulate the cockpit of the Buccaneer.

Entering service with the Navy in 1962, the Buccaneer equipped 700B/700Z, 736, 800, 801, 803 and 809 Naval Air Squadrons. Buccaneers were embarked on *HMS Victorious, Eagle, Ark Royal* and *Hermes*, leaving the service in 1978 following the decommissioning of

and by the time of their celebrated service in the 1991 Gulf War, where they were employed as laser target-designators for British Tornado GR 1's, using the underwing mounted Westinghouse AN/ASQ-153\AN/AVQ-23 Pave Spike pod. They were also fully equipped with the AN/ALQ-101 ECM pod, chaff and flare dispensers, AIM-9 Sidewinder missile and where necessary underwing 'slipper' fuel tanks. Later in the conflict the Buccs also undertook attack missions, designating their own laser guided bombs. The type ended its days with 208 Squadron in 1994, having operated for some years with the Sea Eagle anti-ship missile, which had replaced Martel in 1986.

In January 1963, sixteen aircraft were ordered by the South African Air Force, as the S 50, which was a S 2 with the addition of Bristol Siddeley BS.605 rocket engines. Fifteen entered service, following the loss of one on its delivery flight. Aircraft served from 1965 – 1991.

One of the real classics, the type has certainly not been over-kitted, possibly due to the ready availability of the handful of older toolings. Some in the UK rate 'the Brick' as the finest and most handsome machine ever – certainly more so than its spindly contemporary the Lightning, which is feted on every continent and in every scale - and perhaps it is this close affection that makes us so surprised that the rest of the world is slower to care? We will have to build lots now, and show them how wrong they are.

*Ark Royal.* FAA machines were subsequently transferred to the RAF, which had taken over the maritime strike role,

The first RAF unit to receive the Buccaneer S 2B was 12 Squadron at RAF Honington in 1969, and the type also operated as an integral part of RAF Germany. In 1980 the entire RAF fleet was grounded following a mid-air structural failure, the upshot of which was the refurbishment of sixty selected aircraft, and the UK fleet eked out is service at Lossiemouth. RAF Buccaneers received various upgrades during their service life, keeping pace with new weapons capabilities,

# Pirates Fly

## CMR's Hawker Siddeley Buccaneer S Mk 2/2C/2D

By Paul Janicki

This stout box contains everything you could possibly need to complete a well detailed model of the hefty carrier borne strike aircraft, including all the weapons applicable through its career with the Fleet Air Arm. Options allow folded radome, open weapons bay and airbrakes, and folded wings. Etched parts cater for all the cockpit and external areas, and a masking set for the canopy is included, as is a thirty-five page instruction manual that covers everything you need to build any one of the options possible.

### Construction

Much of the work entails the preparation and careful selection of parts appropriate to the version and colour scheme chosen. The cockpit is the starting point and here you have a choice of seats for either early or late S2s. You also have a choice of pre-painted etched parts for the instrument consoles, which will involve sanding off the resin detail. This also goes for the seat details, straps and other

| TECH PANEL | |
|---|---|
| Scale: 1/72 | Kit No: 1165 |
| Price: £73.99 | Decal Options: 12 |
| Panel Lines: Recessed | Status: New Tooling |
| Type: Resin | Manufacturer: CMR |
| UK Importer: Hannants | US Importer: Squadron |

items around the airframe. When this area is complete, the cockpit assembly, undercarriage bays, tail pipes and weapons bay can be fitted to their respective upper and lower fuselage halves. Here I found the weapons bay to be a poor fit, and I was obliged to model it closed.

Joining the halves entailed some clamping and filling and I was also obliged to use some filler when fitting the nose in the closed position. I turned my attention to the petal dive brakes next. These are fiddly, but with patience a good result was achieved.

The surface detailing is very good with all the vortex generators very finely depicted. The root detailing at the folds is good too but some careful trimming is required to ensure a good fit. I cut down a couple of dressmaking pins to represent the jury struts as they would be stronger than plastic rod or something as suggested in the build diagrams.

I opted for an asymmetric stores fit of one slipper tank and the 'Buddy-Buddy' hose pod, and along with these, the final items I fixed in place were the small and easily damaged parts such as the pitot, antenna arrestor hook and vacform canopy. The canopy features the central framework as a resin part that is fixed to the inside, which will present a challenge to some. The small dividing windshield for

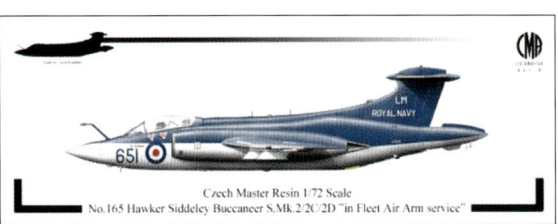

Czech Master Resin 1/72 Scale
No.165 Hawker Siddeley Buccaneer S.Mk.2/2C/2D "in Fleet Air Arm service"

the cockpit crew is also a bit tricky to get to fit but will no doubt reward a careful hand

## Colour Options

There are options for twelve different aircraft or variations, including three in the Extra Dark Sea Grey and White era of the mid 1960s, seven in the overall Grey period with full 'D' type roundels and pale blue serials and all their respective heraldry, and finally two with the later toned-down red/blue roundels but the same serials and stencilling. My choice was for XN982/235 of 801 NAS on HMS *Victorious* 1966. To help with the schemes CMR thoughtfully include what mods, seat types and items are required for each aircraft, and also which underwing stores arrangement would have been fitted with each of the schemes .

## Conclusion

Building this kit wasn't without its problems and frustrations, but on the plus side, the package adds up to a very comprehensive and highly detailed kit and you end up with lots of useful stores and bits to add more detail to older kits of the type, not to mention the equally extensive decal sheets and very full and informative instructions.

Not a kit for the beginner, but certainly a very fine product and one recommended to those able to do it justice.

Perhaps one of the best items currently available to upgrade the Airfix Buccaneer is Neomega's resin cockpit set. Widely known for the quality and detail in their products, Neomega's Brick building set has

**Essential Upgrade: Buccaneer Cockpit Set, Part No: C23, Price: £18.50, Manufacturer: Neograde**

been one of their best sellers, and with little likelihood of an up to date kit of the type in this scale this item is likely to remain a hot commodity. Includes two Martin Baker seats, control panels, main cockpit tub, side panels, canopy console, HUD, and control stick. www.neomega-resin.com

Buccaneer S 2B XV333 of No.208 Squadron based at RAF Lossiemouth. This picture dates to August 1989, and the aircraft was transferred from preservation to the Fleet Air Arm Museum in 1994

# 'Bucc Shots'

**A**llan J Harper delves into his archive and provides a photographic look at the Blackburn Buccaneer in both RAF and Royal Navy service.

'Faster, Lower, Longer' was the motto of the incomparable Blackburn Buccaneer. From Royal Navy to RAF service, the 'Brick' confounded its critics, delighted its crews and provided both the RAF and Royal Navy with an aircraft that could operate at low level, deliver a hefty punch and make it back to an aircraft carrier or airbase.

After the cancellation of both the TSR.2 and F-111K, the RAF eventfully adopted the Buccaneer in 1968, in an ironic move as they had, ten years earlier, rejected Blackburn's B-108 proposal for a supersonic Buccaneer, favouring the TSR.2 to meet its Operational Requirement GOR.339 for a Canberra replacement. RAF aircraft were given various upgrades such as the AN/ALQ-101 ECM Pod, chaff and flare dispensers, Sea Eagle missiles and the American AN/AVQ-23 Pave Spike laser designator pod – with which the Buccaneer gained fame in the 1991 Gulf War.

**Another view of Buccaneer S 1 XK534/683 LM of No.700Z at the 1961 SBAC Show at Farnborough, in a 'dirty' pass**

**Buccaneer S 1 XK534/683 LM of No.700Z Intensive Flying Trial Unit (IFTU) seen here in anti-flash white at the 1961 SBAC Show at Farnborough**

Buccaneer S 2 XN983 of No.12 Squadron, around 1972 wearing the Dark Green and Dark Sea Grey over Light Aircraft Grey undersurfaces

A pair of Buccaneer S 2Bs arrive in the Gulf to designate Paveway bombs for the Tornado force in 1992

Buccaneer S 2 XW529 of the A&AEE Boscombe Down around 1988, and wearing the Dark Green and Dark Sea Grey over Light Aircraft Grey undersurfaces. Note the badge on the tail

Buccaneer S 2B of No.15 Squadron taken shortly before the unit converted to the Tornado in 1983

A nice line-up of No.208 Squadron Buccs at RAF Brize Norton in September 1990

The famous Fox's Head of No.12 Squadron

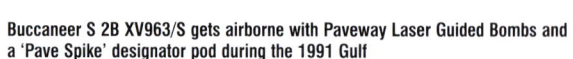

Buccaneer S 2B XV963/S gets airborne with Paveway Laser Guided Bombs and a 'Pave Spike' designator pod during the 1991 Gulf

Buccaneer S 2B XX900 of No.12 Squadron in July 1990. She now resides at Bruntingthorpe

Buccaneer S 2B XW543 in the later grey scheme seen here at RAF Brize Norton in September 1990

Buccaneer S 2B XT277 in the markings of No.237 OCU on display at the Cosford Aerospace Museum in 1992, from where it was later scrapped

'The Bucc Stops Here!' A superb formation of Buccaneers from RAF Lossiemouth formate on a Hercules camera ship to mark the type's retirement in 1994

73

Buccaneer S 2B XV283 of No.237 OCU on detachment at RAF Waddington in 1987

Buccaneer S 2B XV889/MF of No.12 Squadron wearing the wrap-around camouflage scheme of Dark Green and Dark Sea Grey, captured in July 1986 with Martel missiles fitted

A Buccaneer S 2 surrounded by its ground equipment in September 1990

| | |
|---|---|
| | Made in Czech Republic |
| | 1/72nd Scale Aircraft |
| | This page was last updated: 19th April 2012 |
| | "NEW MODEL" |
| | (20th Anniversary) |
| | CMR72-209  Hawker Siddeley Buccaneer S.Mk.2B |
| | "Operation Granby" - 1991 Gulf War |
| | [Two-Seat Low-Level Strike Jet Aircraft] |
| | [Decals, Photo-Etch Detailing Set & Paint Mask Included] |

**TECH PANEL**

Scale: 1/72
Kit No: 72209
Price: £81.60/US$120.59
Type: Resin
Manufacturer: CMR
UK Importer: Hannants
US Importer: Squadron

# Sky Pirate

## CMR's Brick in 1/72

By Ernie Lee

**B**y the time of the 1991 Gulf War the Buccaneer was an old lady. But as the only laser-target marking aircraft with the RAF - being fitted with the AN/AVQ 23E 'Pave Spike' pod, the Buccaneer went out in a blaze of glory.

CMR have produced a number of variants, and this kit includes all the equipment that was carried on the various missions. The company's attention to detail is amazing; the decal sheet covers all twelve aircraft that were involved, including, along with the markings on the 1,000Ib Paveway II Laser-Guided Bomb (seven examples). This includes, I might add, the graffiti!

As I have built this aircraft before with 'everything out', I decided this time to build it as it would be seen at Muharraq prior to a mission, which meant no open nose or folded wings. The machine I chose was XW533/A *Miss Jolly Roger/Fiona/Glenfarcias*, as on the 27th February 1991.

The kit is moulded in light green resin, the fuselage being split horizontally, complete with wings as far as the fold. The first task is the cockpit bath, which itself comes as a complete moulding – side consoles and bulkheads, with rear cockpit instrument panels. You have two options regarding the instruments. You can either leave the original raised detail or remove it and replace with PE parts.

After adding the Martel display and joystick you can concentrate on the ejection seats. These are complete castings with just the thigh guards and PE seat harness to add, and before fitting these in place there is a certain amount of detail to be added to the pilot's position, including the instrument panel, control column and various scoops. With the cockpit in place, minus the seats (because I wanted to show the canopy open and this makes masking easier), there are

just the main wheel well interiors to fit from the inside of the bottom half and the fuselage can be joined and it is here I come up against a problem. On my particular kit there must have been a displacement of the inner section of the mould on the lower port wing, resulting in a large amount of excess resin, which prevented the two halves closing. Resin is soft so half an hour scraping with a curved blade scalpel rectified the situation. This aircraft is definitely a tail sitter so I had to pack as much lead as I could forward of the main wheels before joining the top and bottom.

The engine intake areas are separate items and on this machine the interior is painted the same as the external surfaces, but the lips are stainless steel and the internal part of the lips will need masking. Masking these lips once on the fuselage was going to be tricky, so I decided to paint the interior and then mask the interior line of the lip before cementing them in place.

After adding the nose cone, the next task was the fin and rudder. This is butt-jointed and I tacked it in place with a few spots of PVA to

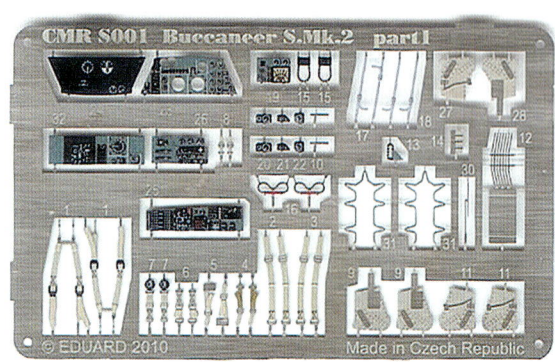

allow removal if the alignment was incorrect. Once satisfied with the position I flooded the joints with super glue.

Outer wing panels came next. I had to modify the hinges slightly to clamp the wings in place before cementing, as it is very easy to get them out of alignment. There are two sets of flaps so that they can be fitted in either the closed or open position. Photographs of these aircraft seemed to show them in the open position, so I did likewise. Again photographic evidence indicates that the air brakes are open when the aircraft is on the ground and fitting them needs care and patience. Oh, and don't forget to fit the flare dispenser first!

I could now add the various antennae etc, but when it came to the ILS Localiser Aerials the thin section at the rear was missing so I had fun drilling out the housing and inserting a short length of wire. The other antennae gave me no trouble, but to protect the 'Violet Picture' Radio Homing Aerials under the nose from being damaged I

temporary cemented a short length of plastic rod into the undercarriage-locating hole.

The model was now ready for painting, and once completed the pre-painted undercarriage was fixed in place and I could add the decals. The weapon load is dependant on the time period. I chose the load noted on 21st of February, which consisted of an AN/ALQ ECM pod, AN/AVQ-21E Pave Spike Laser Designation Pod and two UK 1,000lb Paveway II Laser-Guided Bombs.

One of the last tasks is weathering. Photographs supplied will give you a good idea and in fact around the starboard side under the cockpit it was absolutely scruffy so all you weathering experts can have a field day.

I added the sliding canopy and I now have the pride of my Gulf War collection. This is no 'weekend' construction; but there is a lot of detail, and the kit should keep you occupied for many weeks.

75

# V-Bombers

## Black Buck Vulcan

**T**he Avro Vulcan, the Handly Page Victor and the Vickers Valiant comprised the United Kingdom's strategic nuclear strike force known officially as the V-force or Bomber Command Main Force, which reached its peak in June 1964, with fifty Valiants, seventy Vulcans and thirty nine Victors in service.

### Converting a previously-made Airfix 1/72 Vulcan B 2 into a Black Buck bomber using a Flight Path detail set

By Jan Forsgren

When the Royal Navy took over the strategic deterrent in 1969, the Vulcans were kept flying in front line service, and acted as a strategic reserve. The Vulcan eventually saw action when Argentina invaded the Falkland Islands in the South Atlantic Ocean in 1982. It was decided that bombing missions against the airport in Port Stanley were necessary and to be flown by Vulcans from the Ascension Island in the Atlantic Ocean!

**The first task was to dismantle the original model**

Long before the Falklands War conflict, is was decided that the Vulcan fleet would be disbanded in the early-1990s, and that process had already started when they were urgently needed to perform a very difficult bombing mission. Aerial refueling was practiced as it had not been used for years, and the equipment to release iron bombs had to be reinstalled, much of which was found on airfield dumps!

Vulcan B 2, XM607, was one of the Vulcans that had been fitted with uprated Olympus 301 engines. It was originally intended to carry the American Skybolt nuclear missile, and was selected for *Operation Corporate* use. After removing the 44 Sqn markings and repainting the white undersides with matt Dark Sea Grey, it was flown to Wideawake airfield on Ascension, together with four other Vulcans, escorted by Victor K 2 tankers, each Vulcan requiring two in-flight refuellings during the ferry flight, and arrived on 29 April 1982.

On each strike mission, code-named 'Black Buck', two Vulcans were used, one as primary aircraft and one as the backup. On the very first mission on 30 April, XM607 was flying as the backup, and when the primary aircraft had to abort when a cabin window would not seal properly, XM607 took over and successfully completed the mission.

The raid covered 12,000 kilometers and lasted almost sixteen hours. The bombs were released at 10,000 feet, diagonally across the runway, and one of the twenty-one 1,000lb bombs hit the target. This aircraft flew one more Black Buck mission, this time releasing the bombs at 16,000feet, but none hit the target.

After the two Black Buck raids, XM607 was flown back to Waddington twice and back to Wideawake, and finally back to Waddington on 14 June. It was retired on 21 December 1982..

### Modelling XM607 in 1/72

The Airfix Vulcan B 2 kit originates from the late-1970s, and has been re-released fairly frequently, including currently, as plans to feature

The axles on the landing gear were replaced with piano wire

Lead was added to prevent tail-sitting

A plastic card strip was inserted to fill the gap

Work under way on the bomb bay interior

77

the kit in a special 25th Anniversary have been announced, so there should be no problem obtaining one.

It is accurate enough to make into an acceptably good model. The airframe consists of a fuselage split horizontally with a separate tail cone, upper and lower wing halves, although the detailing might not be quite up to today's standards, with miles of raised panel lines.

Flightpath have produced three detail sets for the Vulcan, one to convert it into a B 1, a detail set for the B 2, and finally a set to convert it to the tanker version.

## Preparing the kit

When I started this project, it was from an already built kit, originally built some years earlier. I started carefully, with a knife, separating the whole model into its original pieces. That was fairly easy as old styrene cement makes this plastic brittle in the joints, but in the process some plastic disappeared and care had to be taken when rebuilding it. The landing gear with all the wheels was a sad affair, but

in the end I saved enough of the wheels to reconstruct them and replaced the axles on the landing gears with piano wire.

## Construction

I did not pay too much attention to the cockpit interior, apart from replacing the original seats with white metal ones from Aeroclub, as very little of it is visible from the outside. All the interior was painted black and dry brushed with grey. The rear crew porthole windows were drilled open as they are missing in the kit.

From the lower fuselage entry hatch, you are able to see some of the interior, so I added the forward bulkhead, a floor and an internal ladder to the lower fuselage half. In front of the bulkhead I inserted some lead to prevent a tail-sitter.

I decided to show the bomb bay open, as I had a photograph showing it in detail. In the kit you have the option of closing the bay or installing the Blue Steel with the corresponding bay door piece. In the lower fuselage half the engine air intakes were placed and glued

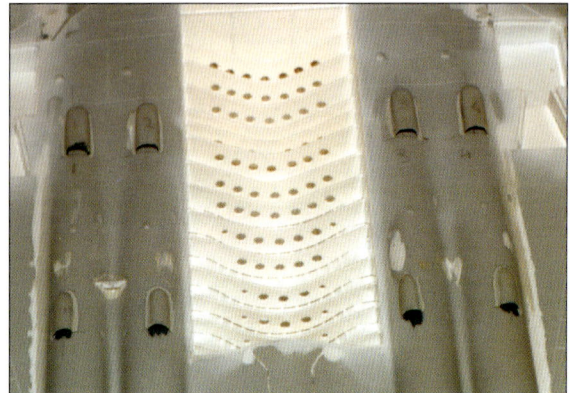

Detail added into the bomb bay

The mainwheel well doors were made from 0.2mm sheet brass

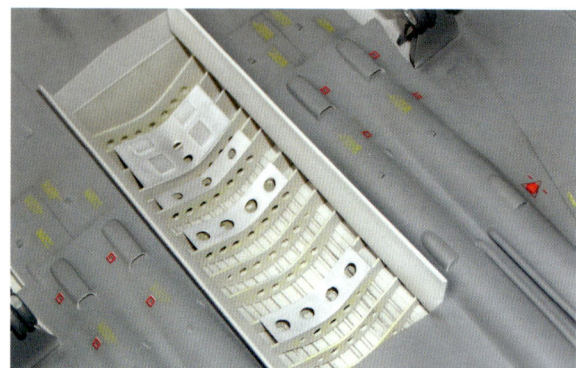

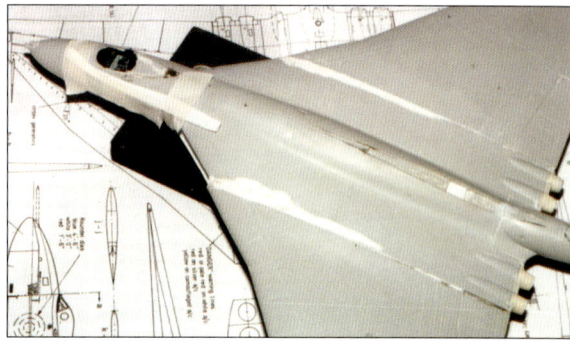

The kit's engine exhausts were exchanged with DB Resin items

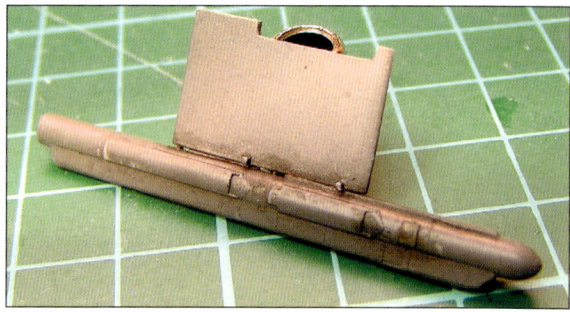

The jamming pod and the pylons were also painted Dark Sea Grey

and the fuselage halves were assembled. In the accompanying photograph, a plastic card strip between the two fuselage halves is visible, necessary because there was material missing.

For the bomb bay interior, I used a large 0.5mm Plasticard sheet, on which I attached several thin styrene strips at equal distance. I inserted the bomb bay upper surface through the hole and glued it against the inside of the upper fuselage half, following the upper fuselage curvature.

Walls were made in 1mm Plasticard, making the fuselage center section very rigid. Now I could measure the thirteen stringers that had to be prepared individually. This operation was very rewarding and I am pleased with the end result – even though I didn't finish the work and manage to load it with the twenty-one bombs. I plan to do this some day.

The wings were assembled and attached to the fuselage. Lots of effort had to be made lining the inside of the air intakes with Plasticard to get rid of the mould seams.

Before attaching the fin, all the raised panel lines on the fuselage and wings, and the fin, were sanded down and their positions marked on with a sharp lead pencil. Although there are several scale drawings of the Vulcan around today, I personally used the drawings made by F J Henderson, plus some reference photographs from various books and magazines. The new engraved panel lines were made with a sharpened Bare-Metal Scriber, using a metal ruler. For rounded surfaces Dymo tape was used.

At the rear, the original engine exhausts were exchanged with DB Resin items, and then the fin was attached to the fuselage.

The wheel wells should have been detailed, but I had no specific information at the time of the model's reconstruction, and simply

Plasticard lining was added to the inside of the gear doors

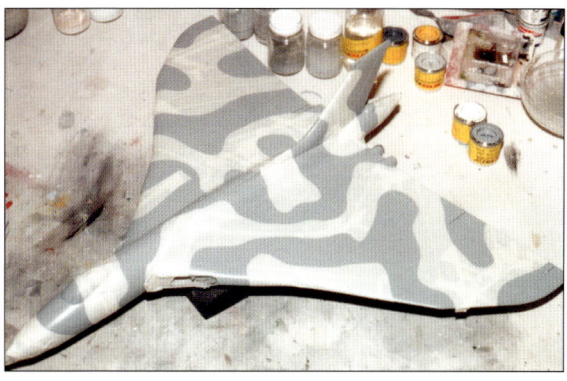

Masking and painting the camouflage on the upper surface

resorted to gluing the landing gear in them. However the model does stand very nicely on the original kit landing gear, perfectly symmetrical.

When the Vulcans were prepared for the flight to the South Atlantic, they were made to carry both AGM-45 Shrike missiles and the ALQ-101 jamming pod from the Buccaneer, as their original equipment was outdated and useless. The pylons were attached to the hardpoints where the American Skybolt nuclear missile would have been carried, had it not been cancelled.

These pylons are included in the kit, specifically for the Black Buck raid option, and although they are not exactly like the real ones, they look good enough. The extra gadget, which the jamming pod was attached to was made from sheet styrene and the pod came from the Hasegawa weapons set. It's actually a modified AN/ALQ-119, and looks very like the Buccaneer jamming pod. On the Black Buck raids they only carried the jamming pod, (apart from the twenty-one 1,000lb bombs in the bomb bay of course); Shrike missiles were to be carried on other attack missions.

The crude kit ladder was exchanged with PP Aeropart's delicate photo-etched access ladder, and glued to the inside of the hatch. An etched brass ladder is also included in Flight Path's new sets for the Vulcan.

## Painting and Decals

Xtracolor Dark Green and Medium Sea Grey were used for the upper surfaces and Dark Sea Grey for the lower surfaces. The jamming pod and the pylons were also painted Dark Sea Grey.

A wash of white spirit and black oil paint, with dry pastels for the final weathering were applied, sealed with Johnsons Klear/Future, mixed with some Tamiya Flat Base. The decals were mainly the Airfix kit's originals with some from Modeldecal Set 71.

It was an interesting experience building this old kit, and I am very pleased with the result.

# Airfix make it Easy – The Vickers Valiant

### Airfix's new kit in 1/72

By Ted Taylor

**1:72 VICKERS VALIANT BK.Mk.1**
**TECH PANEL**

Scale: 1/72

Kit No: 11001

Type: Injection Moulded Plastic

Manufacturer: Airfix

Available from www.luckymodel.com

## He who would Valiant Be

This is the kit that nobody expected to see in injection moulded form. I have heard the words 'insignificant', 'not enough likely sales' etc. etc. many times over the years but Hornby changed all that and at last we have a full set of 'V' bombers.

The Valiant was the first of the V force as a result of a Government requirement for a long range, high speed bomber. The design from Vickers was at first rejected but with modifications and speed of production promises, was finally accepted and three prototypes were contracted in 1949, which were being built and assembled at Foxwarren experimental shop. The final assembly began in 1951 and the first flight lifted off from the grass runway in May of 1951. Later flight trials were conducted at Hurn airport on concrete runways. The aircraft was officially named Valiant after an earlier Vickers biplane but was later destroyed by a fire in the wing while on trials in 1952.

Eventually four types of Valiant entered service. The B Mk 1 bomber, B.(PR) reconnaissance, B(K) tanker, and a recon /tanker version. There was a B Mk 2 prototype built and shown at Farnborough' in 1954 and christened 'the Black Bomber' to be used at low level as a pathfinder. This had a revised undercarriage and lengthened fuselage but was never proceeded with.

An OCU was established at Gaydon airfield in 1954 (Now the home of Historic Cars Museum) to train pilots, and between then and 1956 the Valiants travelled to many parts of the globe on tests and goodwill trips.

In October of 1956 the aircraft dropped Britain's first atomic bomb on Maralinga Australia for radiation tests. A few weeks later all the squadrons moved to Malta where they were engaged in the Suez campaign and thus the Valiant was the first and only V bomber to drop bombs in anger until that lone raid on Port Stanley with the Vulcan in 1982.

1957 saw the dropping of Britain's first H bomb on Christmas Island in Operation Grapple by 49 Sqn. By 1964 it was realised that low level attacks were less risky than high level approaches to targets so the planes were camouflaged in the standard RAF scheme and began new tactics, but the strain on the wing spars was too great and the whole fleet showed signs of stress and breakages. Rather than repair the Air Ministry decided to scrap the whole lot with the exception of the example now in the RAF Museum at Cosford.

## There's no Discouragement

The kit comes in a very large box and when you see the length of the fuselage you will understand why. It is moulded in a grey plastic, which seems very easy to work with for sanding etc. The top half of

The cockpit straight from the box. The nature of the canopy means little is visible once assembled, so this level of detail will probably satisfy most builders

The finished crew compartment with seats added. Simple but effective

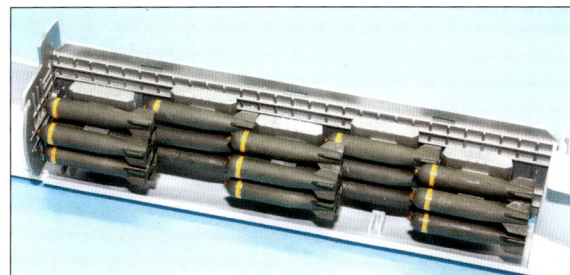

Two alternative weapons loads are provided for the nicely detailed bomb bay. Here the twenty-one 1,000lb conventional bombs have been loaded

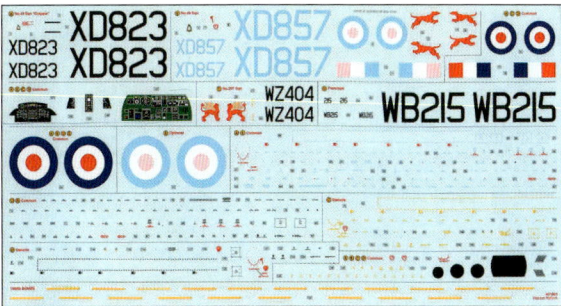

The kit's decal sheet is impressive, offering complete stencilling for both schemes

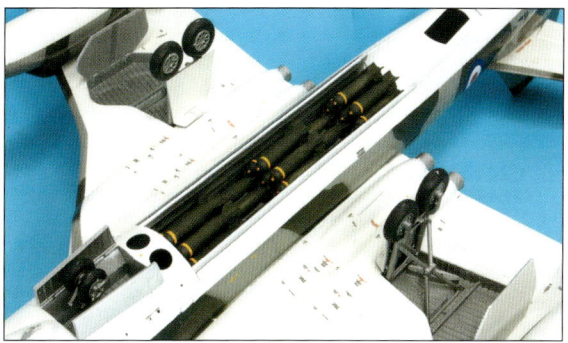

The underside of the completed model showing the loaded weapons bay and main gear compartments

the shoulder-mounted wing is a one-piece item and although the fuselage halves may look flimsy they have fairly thick walls and large locating pins so when all the internal structures are in place you have a very solid model. Surface detail is minimal with sharp panel lines but the real plane was fully flush riveted so it looks reasonable.

The cockpit is fairly basic with decals for instrument panels and five nicely detailed seats for pilots and crew. Only the pilots have ejection seats and the crew bale out the door if in trouble. Airfix have thoughtfully provided two internal weapons loads with two bomb bay fittings, one carries the A bomb and the other carries an impressive twenty-one 1,000lb conventional bombs. You also get to choose where you position the air deflector behind the bay.

The clear sprue gives alternative canopies and bomb aimer's areas and a strange item that I could find no use for. There are poseable elevators on the tailplanes and the ailerons can be deflected, but no movable flaps.

The fit of the parts is excellent, with no filler required anywhere, and all that is needed is a quick rub down of the joins to remove any blemishes. In fact my wings and tailplanes are not cemented at all and the join looks like a panel line. Even the canopies have a very large tight locating tab, which means even the clumsiest hand will not get cement on them.

The decal sheet is all in register and the colours are strong even over the camouflage. Four aircraft are covered on the sheet, and all arc arranged in groups making it easy to sort each type. The instruction booklet covers everything very simply so even the youngest modeller can handle it with ease and a great big sheet comes with positions for all the stencils.

The Hornby/Airfix team have really done their homework on this one, so keep up the good work. This was one of the easiest models I have built recently. Airfix make it easy and affordable - unlike some of their competition.

I have no good reliable drawings to check accurate dimensions but my eye tells me this is certainly a Vickers Valiant.

Vickers Valiant at Bristol Filton Airport, some time in the early sixties (Adrian Pingstone)

The completed model captures the low-slung weighty feel of the aircraft to perfection

# Black Buck Victor

## Matchbox's 1/72 Victor as a 'Black Buck' tanker using Flight Path's detail set

By Jans Forsgren

Conceived as one of Britain's V-Force bombers, the Victor ended its life as a tanker and saw action in both the Falklands conflict and in the Gulf War, and was finally retired in 1993. Victors of Nos 55 and 57 Squadrons were deployed to Ascension Island during the Falklands conflict. The work of the Victor tankers provided the foundation of the successful operations from Ascension Island and brought the Victor back firmly into the public eye.

During the first Black Buck bombing raid on the landing strip at Port Stanley, eleven Victors accompanied a single Vulcan on the 7,000nm flight, taking turns to refuel the Vulcan and each other. Some Victors had to stay longer with the Vulcan whilst others returned to Ascension, took on more fuel, and met the Vulcan and Victors on their return to Ascension Island.

XL192 was chosen as the subject of my model. It flew to Wideawake on 18 April 1982. On 20/21 April, XL192 was airborne for 14 hrs 45 mins and covered 6,500nm, piloted by Sqn Ldr J G Elliott, setting a new record for the longest ranging operational reconnaissance mission. This was also one of the K 2s that followed Vulcan XM607 on both the trip to Ascension and on the first Black Buck mission.

XL192 returned to Marham in July 1982 and was scrapped in February 1996.

To me, the Victor represents aircraft thinking of the 1950s: big, bold and… beautiful! Seeing this aircraft with its large tail is like seeing an old dinosaur.

## Modelling the Victor Tanker

The old 1/72 Matchbox Victor, recently given a new lease of life by Revell, is still a very good kit, but of course far from the state-of-the-art standards that are produced today. Overall measurements seem good enough, and it's a lot of plastic! In my case in white, grey and dark green as it was from the original Matchbox issue.

The level of detailing is minimal and to make a representative model will take some time and effort. My main reference was, as for the Vulcan, a set of drawings by Arthur L Bentley in *Scale Aviation Modeller International*, August 2006, Vol 12/8, which I enlarged to 1/72. There are also scale drawings in *Warpaint No 26* and I also have the old *Aeroguide No 11*.

Flight Path's Victor K 2 set, with white-metal cones for the tailplane and some etched brass to enhance the in-flight refueling equipment, was purchased, (the current detail set also has engine air intakes in resin with control vanes in etched brass and looks very good). And of course there was the brass framing for the cockpit glazing. The frame looked beautiful with small rivets and lots of detail, and was used.

## Fuselage

Martin Baker Mk 3 white metal ejection seats from Aeroclub replaced the kit's originals, but apart from these, all the original kit parts were used, as the view into the cockpit is very limited. I had no clue of how much weight to put in the nose to prevent making it a tail sitter, so that had to wait.

To strengthen the fuselage join I cut strips of sheet styrene and glued them alternately to each half. When joining the two halves these tabs will self-align the parts and reduce the amount of subsequent sanding considerably, and it will also strengthen the fuselage joint.

The longitudinal panel lines were rescribed before joining the fuselage halves, then the fuselage halves were glued together and after treating the joint with Milliput, the panel lines around the fuselage were scribed, along with the rest of the kit where necessary.

The wing attachment areas were now prepared, and here some work was needed to get a good fit, due to Matchbox's very unusual design, with the wing connecting to the fuselage in a recess. Wing spars were made from strong plastic tubes, but brass tubes would have been even better, and the wing was strengthened further with lateral stringers in the front, as it felt very weak there. Wing spars are necessary on most models, as too much strain is put on the fuselage

Panel lines around the fuselage were rescribed, along with the rest of the kit where necessary

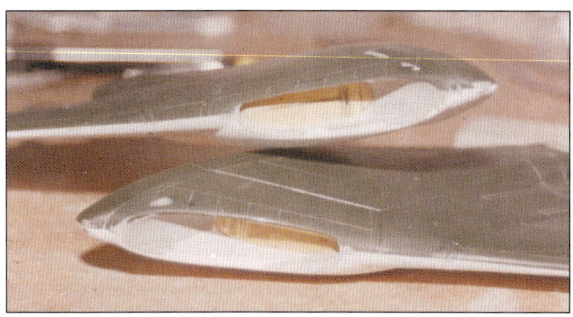

The lower lip was extended slightly downwards with Milliput and all the inside was lined with sheet styrene

Wing spars were made from strong plastic tubes

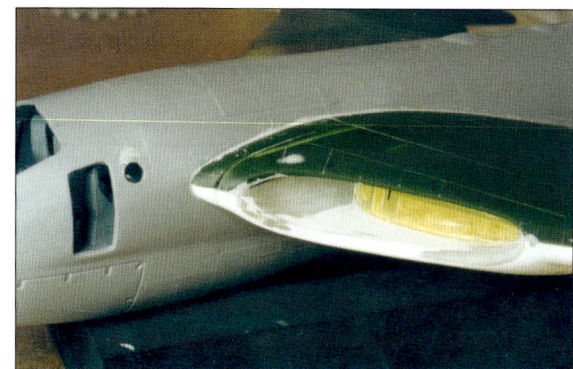

The photo-etch covers were used as a guide to make new parts

joints otherwise, when handling it during construction. At the time I built this Victor I had no pictures of extended air brakes and decided to glue them in the closed position. Milliput was applied and everything was sanded flush, the contours along the air brakes were scribed and new strakes were made from sheet styrene.

## Wings

The engine air intakes are difficult to improve as there is a plethora of guide vanes inside that are virtually impossible to install. The lower lip was extended slightly downwards with Milliput and all the inside was lined with sheet styrene.

The photo-etch covers in the accompanying photo were only used to have something to model the intake shape after, as new covers were made later.

The guide vane closest to the opening, which is the only visible guide vane when the FOD covers are used, was replaced with a more correct one.

The wings have a 'kink' where the inner and outer wing panels are joined, but this was not present on the kit and had to be corrected. Study photos thoroughly before doing this.

I chose to model the flaps in the extended position and some rails from strips and rods were added for the extension mechanism. The wings were attached to the fuselage and everything looked good, but later a former RAF mechanic told me the wing tips with the pitot tubes should be angled slightly downwards. This can be seen on photographs of the real aeroplane, but I missed it!

The rear end of the faired-in wing tanks had to be cut off and modified to fit the extended flaps – this is something Matchbox missed. The hose drum units were detailed with photo-etched parts, the propeller in front and folded 'basket' in the rear. Close to the wing root there is a wing fence, and by using a razor saw a thin slot was made into which a 0.25mm sheet styrene was glued and shaped to fit.

## Tailplane

The fin was thinned by sanding the surfaces and scribing in the panel lines. When aligning the tailplane, it is necessary to place the model horizontally on the modelling bench and keep the fin absolutely

vertical. A symmetrical airframe is vital, and for adjusting the tail it is better to use slow curing liquid glue than CA glue.

The stabilizers were attached on top of the fin at the marked dihedral according to photographs; this required some Milliput and lots of work, mainly because the kit parts don't fit very well. Flight Path's white-metal cones on the back and front of the tailplane replaced the original cones. Wing fences were made on the stabilizers with the same method as the on the main wing.

The model was now almost complete and it was time to check for the necessary nose weight by balancing the model on the piano wire struts that were temporarily representing the main gear. One bottle of CA glue, or 25 grammes, was needed and the appropriate amount of lead was inserted through a hole made in the underside of the front fuselage and glued into the nose with epoxy glue. It was quite easy to cover the hole and apply some Milliput and all traces of the operation were gone.

## Cockpit canopy No 1

Now to the nerve-wracking part of this story! The photo-etched canopy framing was formed into a cylindrical shape over a tube of the

83

Slow-curing liquid glue was used to allow accurate placing of the tail fin

Flight Path's white-metal cones on the back and front of the tailplane replaced the kit parts

Establishing the necessary weight in the nose

The etched canopy frame part looks excellent but was problematic to fit

The etched frame was faired in with a little Milliput and looked excellent

right size, but the problem is that the Victor's canopy is a double curvature which is impossible to obtain unless heating, cutting and soldering the brass, but I could live with this simplified canopy as the framing was beautiful.

The next obstacle was to find some thin 'window' plastic. I eventually found a suitable piece and glued the plastic film to the photo-etched framing, (already pre-painted), and installed it all in the fuselage with CA glue. Some Milliput and it all looked beautiful, except a small problem in profile because of the omission of the double curvature.

It stayed like that for a week, but then the windows cracked! I did it all again with some other window material and this time it lasted for three weeks and then I gave up.

At this stage the model was painted and almost ready, but it's not the first time I have had to change course completely during a build. I have repainted several models when I was unhappy with something – it's never too late to improve.

### Cockpit canopy No 2

The thick, terrible-looking original canopy was retrieved from the scrap box and thinned down from the inside, polished and dipped in Johnsons Klear/Future and glued against the sheet styrene fuselage rim – as I had to build up the fuselage after the brass frame experience

The fuselage and canopy were sanded flush and polished to a beautiful shine!

The locations of the glass panels were measured, and the framing covered by Tamiya tape strips; then the glass panels could be masked. When all panels were covered, the tape over the framing was removed and all could be painted.

Why didn't I do this from the beginning, the result was perfect!

### Landing gear

The landing gear is all made from non-modified kit items, with only one small photo-etched part. When testing the landing gear, the model sat perfectly with the wing tips at equal height. The undercarriage legs are sturdy enough to carry the weight of the model. Details such as hydraulic lines and connecting links were added to the wheel wells.

The canopy was glued into place and filler applied to the cracks

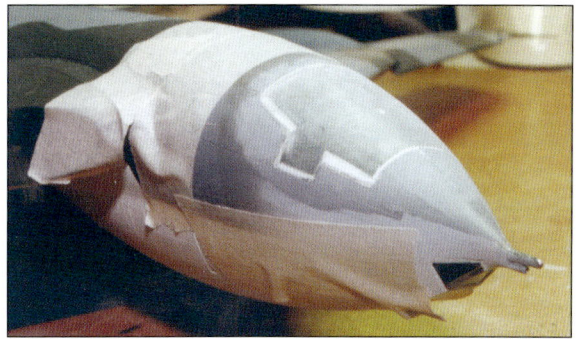

The canopy and fuselage were sanded flush for a perfect fit

Polished back to clarity, the result is spectacular

Canopy frame masking underway

This was an excellent solution, and the finished canopy is a perfect fit

## Detailing

The kit ram air intakes for the turbines in front of the fin were too simple, and simply had to be replaced. Holes in the fuselage were cut, and new intakes were modelled from sheet styrene, and finally there was a photo-etched part for the front end. Tabs were glued on the inside of the fuselage and painted black, and the new intakes were glued to the tabs after painting the fuselage. There were many small blade antennas and air inlet holes added, all of which were found on detail photos. Covers for the engine air inlets were made from sheet styrene, trimmed to fit and painted bright red.

## Painting and decals

Painting was done after the first cockpit canopy attempt, and was completed after the final canopy was fitted. Ordinary drafting tape was used for the sharp demarcation lines between the different colours.

The standard paint scheme was Dark Green and Medium Sea Grey upper surfaces with white undersides – all painted with Xtracolor paint. Before applying the decals the whole model was airbrushed with a few thin coats of Johnson's Klear/Future, which was repeated after the decals were set.

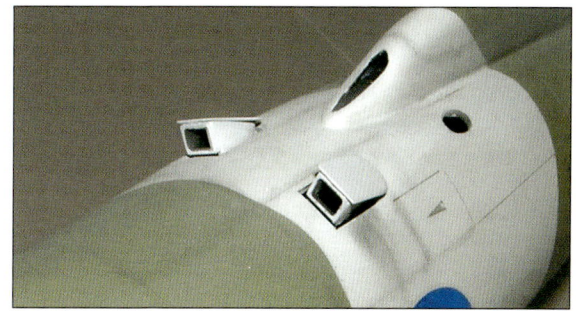

New intakes were fitted after painting the fuselage

Decals are mostly the original kit decals, which actually were very good in spite of their age. The roundels were replaced with Modeldecal items, because they had already been used in the first build of the kit.

Finally I applied a wash of white spirit and dark brown oil color that was sealed with Klear/Future mixed with Tamiya Flat Base. For the final weathering, dry pastel powder and a small brush were used on the satin surface.

I'm glad I finally built this monster aircraft, and looking at it in my model cabinet is rewarding. I'm also pleased to say that my Victor won a Highly Commended and the Handley Page Trophy at IPMS(UK) Scale Modelworld and scored wins at both the Swedish and Norwegian IPMS National Shows.

85

# Chapter 9

# TSR 2 – The Lost Potential

## Great Expectations

By Gary Hatcher (Historical Introduction By Tim Large)

**While Tiny Tim gorged on goose, Gary Hatcher repaired to a draughty attic with a test shot of the Airfix TSR 2 and had an anti-flash white Christmas**

The TSR 2 (Tactical Strike/Reconnaissance) started life in 1954 when the Air Staff began looking for a replacement for the Canberra (TSR.1). When in 1957 the Conservative government cancelled the Avro 730 strategic bomber, a new specification was issued, GO 339, which was itself finalised a year later as OR343. The Government would not place a contract with a single manufacturer, only with a group of firms working together as they intended an amalgamation of the aircraft industry into BAC.

In 1958 the Air Ministry, along with the Ministry of Aviation, pressed Vickers Armstrong and English Electric into a composite design, with the announcement on 1 January 1959 that they would build the aircraft. The formation of BAC took place in February 1960, however because of the upheaval, it was not until October that year that the division of work between Vickers Armstrong and English Electric for the TSR 2 was settled.

Along with the massive work effort, a Government bureaucracy containing upwards of 60 committees evolved. In theory subcontractors would work through BAC, who would deal with the Ministry. In practice it was a disaster, subcontractors would deal with the Government, with no contact with BAC, who in turn could not change any aspect of the design without going through the administration. On top of this, the Ministry of Aviation wanted complete control over the project, as did the Treasury and the resulting infighting would sap at the TSR 2 until its termination in 1965.

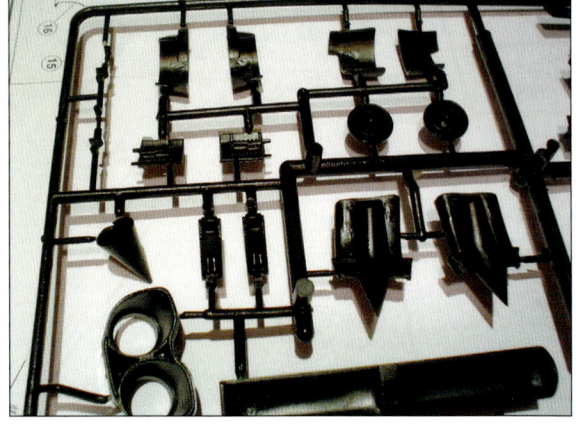

**Some of the components, including intakes and trunking**

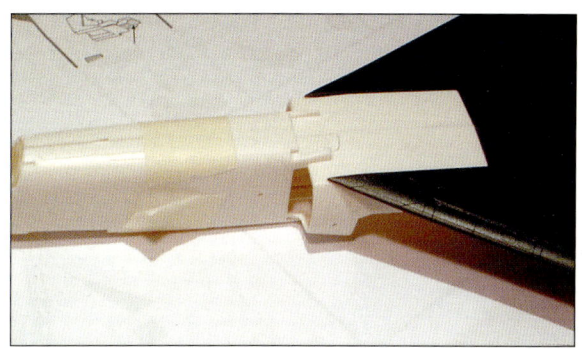

The wing assembly promises to be an excellent fit

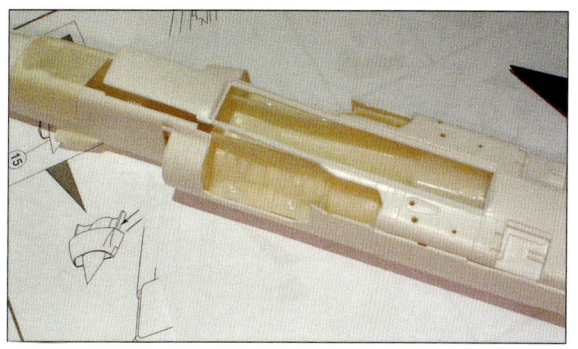

The lower fuselage section slots neatly over the insert

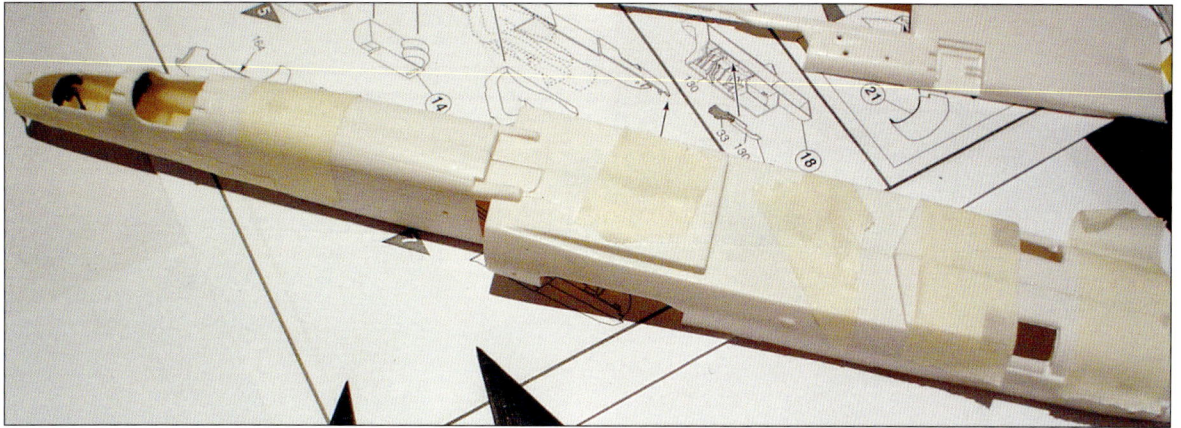

Airfix have designed the kit with refreshingly few visible fuselage seams

In 1958 the Royal Navy refused to have any thing to do with TSR 2, opting for Blackburn's NA.39 (Buccaneer) as their new strike aircraft. The purchase of Polaris from the USA in 1963 and the unsuccessful attempt at selling the TSR 2 to the Australians further undermined the project, and the last blow was the newly elected Labour Government's decision at the start of 1965 to opt for around 150 of the much less capable American F-111A.

Despite of the appalling mismanagement, on the 30 September 1964 the TSR 2 made it's first flight, one year behind schedule. Problems had been encountered with the undercarriage and the engines, but these were soon resolved, and the aircraft first went supersonic on its fourteenth flight. By the end of the initial testing, including low level runs, the TSR 2 had surpassed all expectations. But on 6 April 1965, with three aircraft built and 17 on the assembly line, the axe came (as it did for the HS.681 and P.1154). Work and testing was stopped. BAC were instructed to destroy all aircraft, jigs and documents etc, and thus the end came for the TSR 2 – by far the world's most advanced and capable military aircraft of its time and for decades to come.

## Cutting To The Quick

Receiving a carrier bag of different coloured sprues, accompanied by a sheaf of photocopied instructions and neither decals or box may not be everyone's idea of an ideal Christmas present, but when it constitutes an early preview of the year's most talked about kit, and the instructions are annotated in the hand of Mr Trevor Snowden, a chap is liable to look up and take notice. Thus, after collecting the goods in a foggy exchange with a colleague at Ferrybridge Services, I scuttled home and spent until three in the morning in a state of almost narcotic hypnosis gluing them together. It was a couple of days before Christmas 2005. The deadline for publication was very early in January, so with all manner of seasonal visits and journeys on the calendar, I had to get my skates on.

Before continuing in this vein, allow me to interject a couple of points. Firstly, this is a test shot. While releasing such an item for

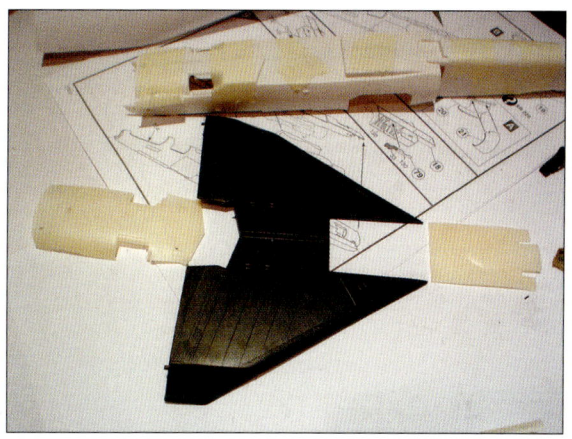

The three-part upper-fuselage assembly is a nice piece of engineering

review suggests a degree of confidence on the part of the manufacturer, it would be unfair of me to present it as other than a very early pre-production test shot, and therefore I will comment little on the fit of the parts, but rather attempt to give an idea of what the final production kit promises to be like. Secondly, and for the benefit of those few readers who haven't already skipped the bulk of these ramblings to discover my conclusion, it is a very good model, and the final version promises to be even better.

## Cutting Even Quicker

I am a dreadful modeller. It takes me months to build anything, so I had to work quickly to get this finished in time. Fortunately Airfix facilitate the task with the engineering of the kit. Both top and bottom are designed in such a way as to leave minimal seams to clean up, and the whole main undercarriage bay assembly – even at this early stage in its genesis – was a good tight fit.

Most of the pieces present were cast in a hard disagreeable plastic, either black or cream in colour, which ignored liquid poly completely, and only reacted favourably to superglue. Needless to say the

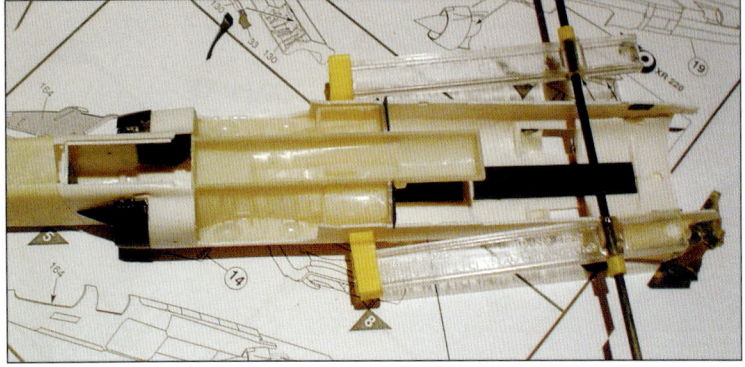

A Berni-clamp is ideal to secure the curved sides of the bomb bay

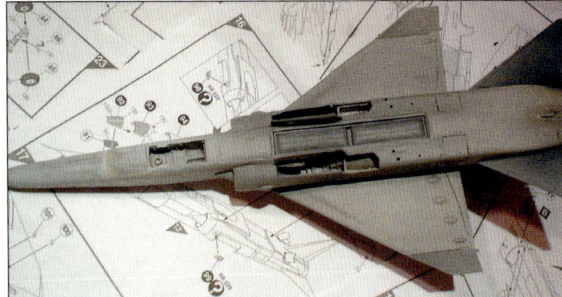

Underside of assembled aircraft

The tail and upper airbrakes

Humbrol Matt White was airbrushed onto the smaller undercarriage components

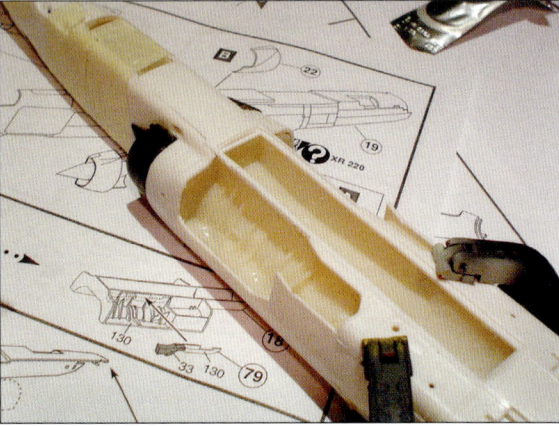

A tight fit was achieved in this area with no problem

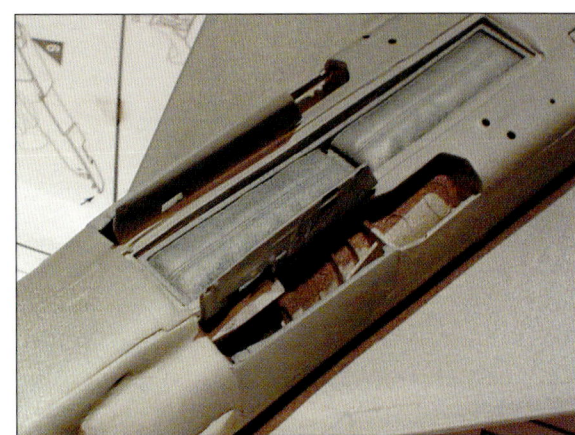

A closer look at the lower-middle section fully assembled

production kit will be a different kettle of fish. Panel lines are crisp and tidy, and easily on a par with anything from other mainstream manufacturers. The test shot featured a number of lines that were engraved erroneously – so disregard any anomalies you may see in this department. The moulds have been polished too, so the surface of the kit parts is smooth, and easy to work on.

Construction starts with filling the fuselage up with undercarriage bays and cockpit tubs. The former feature nice moulded detail, while the latter will be provided with decals for the instrument panels and side consoles. As little enough is visible through the aircraft's canopy, and time was short, I simply painted the cockpit interior grey and fell to wassailing instead.

Once the various inserts were applied I joined the fuselage halves,

taking care to line up the cockpit apertures to ensure the best possible fit of the transparencies. Everything slotted nicely into place, and in fact the only parts of the whole kit that were in any way controversial were the intakes and associated trunking, which I am informed are to be re-engineered prior to production.

Addition of the wing and upper fuselage sections was most satisfying. Nothing is more intolerable than trying to remove a fuselage seam on a white-painted aeroplane. On this kit you will have only the short section between the wing and the cockpit to worry about!

## Cutting Edge

Things had moved quickly so far, and thanks to the layout and design of the parts I had a finished airframe in only two sessions at the workbench. My usual sanding and filling followed, and Halford's primer was thrown into the mix. It is impossible to say how much filler will be needed on the production kit, but I used neither more nor less than usual on this example, and found that on the whole it

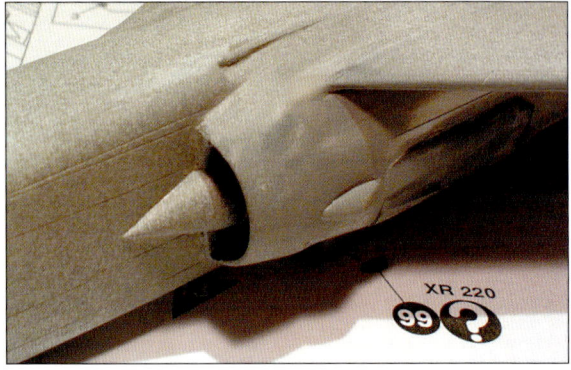

Port intake assembly

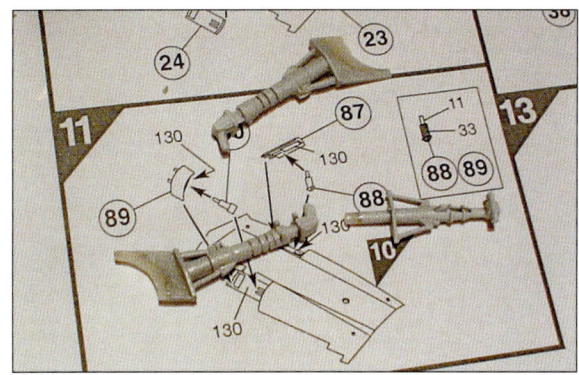

Main gear legs undergoing painting

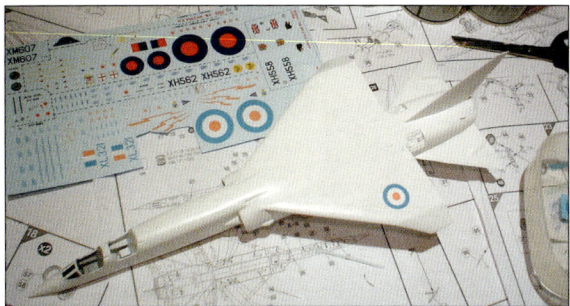

Decalling under way. The instructions promise a mass of stencilling and wing walk details

Halfords acrylics were used for the main airframe

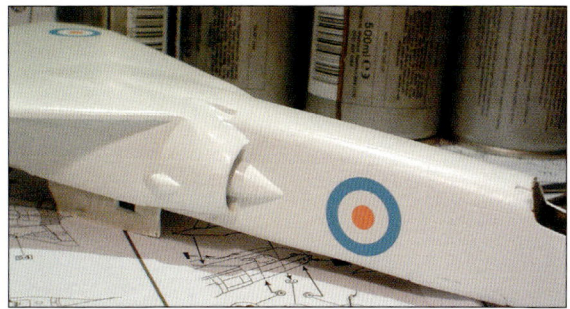

Low-viz roundel applied to starboard fuselage side for effect

Finishing off the wheels with a wash of black oil paint

went together with little fuss. One particularly nice area is the jet pipe assembly, which features good detail and fits beautifully.

The instructions provided suggest that the kit will feature options for three aircraft – all white unsurprisingly. These will be XR219, XR220 and XR222. Comprehensive stencilling will be provided, and the instruction sheet shows some 70 items requiring placement on a finished model. Having no decals, I opted to use parts from an Airfix Vulcan sheet, which were the only anti-flash options I had in my spares box. The roundels for the upper wings seemed about right, but having none of the correct size for the fuselage I applied an outsize example to one side only, in order to give a better idea of what the model will look like when decaled.

The aircraft was finished with numerous coats of Halford's Appliance White, apart from the undercarriage, which I sprayed Humbrol matt white. With hindsight I would have been better airbrushing the whole thing, as the Halford's coats had to be sprayed outside, and repeated snowstorms interrupted the procedure with monotonous regularity.

## In Conclusion

There has been a lot of speculation over this kit. It has, of course, suffered some delay, and this has been due to the manufacturer's determination to get it right. I would be inclined to say, on the

strength of this test shot, that this is precisely what is going to happen. My own inclination is to judge a kit first and foremost by the amount of scratchbuilding I have to waste time doing. Here there are no major sins of omission, and the modeller has a complete aircraft ready to build with no holes to fill, and a more than adequate canvas for superdetailing should one be so inclined.

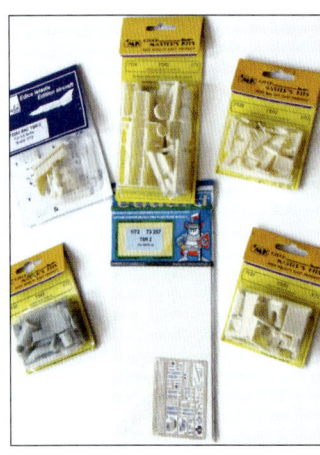

## TECH PANEL

Scale: 1/72

Price: OOP

Kit No: 07004

Type: Injection Moulded Plastic

Manufacturer: Airfix

### ALSO USED:

CMK #7131: TSR 2 Interior set

CMK #7132 TSR 2 Exterior Set

CMK #7133 TSR 2 Control Surfaces

CMK #7134 TSR 2 Bomb Bay and Wheel Wells

Eduard #ED73257 TSR 2 Pre-painted Detail set

# Updating the Legend

### Building the Airfix 1/72 TSR 2 with all the trimmings

By Tony Gloster

There was a great deal of anticipation, when Airfix announced their plans to release a TSR 2. The kit came and went, and while some regard it lacking in detail in certain areas, the overall shape was very pleasing and provides a perfect canvas for some super detailing. In due course a number of after-market sets have become available from the likes of CMK, Pavla and Eduard. As this build is confined to just one TSR 2 the major new parts used are from the four CMK sets, with help from some of the other items available at the time.

Before I start the build, I think it would be a good time to recap on what Airfix provided us with in the box. Inside there are ninety-seven parts moulded in white plastic on five sprues, plus a sealed bag of four clear parts. All the panel lines were recessed, with no flash to speak of. The clear parts had some sink marks, and were very thick, with the framing being ill-defined on all the three parts that made up the canopy. There is a full decal sheet and a set of Airfix's normal clear and precise pictorial style instructions, made up of ten pages. Colour call outs are in Humbrol numbers only, although given the simplicity of the scheme this should prove uncontroversial.

### The Resin and Etched sets

CMK were quick off the mark, producing four sets for the TSR 2, to date. These are Cockpit, Wheel and Bomb Bay, Control Surfaces and an Exterior set, which includes engine inlets. The resin mouldings are, as you may expect, very good and in the cockpit set there are two etched sheets by Eduard, as well as a three-piece vacform canopy to round off the package.

Joining in the party, Pavla have produced a cockpit set, which is a much simpler affair than the CMK set, although that does not detract from the quality of the resin and it features some very nice details, especially the seats, which are available separately. Finally we come to Eduard's contribution, which takes the form of a pre-painted etched set, which is comprehensive in its scope and will keep anyone who enjoys working with this medium very happy indeed.

### Construction

The first thing to do was to decide on just what I would replace, and which sets I would use. The most obvious candidates were the cockpit, bomb bay and main wheel wells. For the cockpit there was a choice as to which resin set to use, and in the end the CMK set won out, because I wanted to show the canopies open, and it had parts to

The after-market sets, by CMK, Pavla and Eduard, cover all aspects of the kit

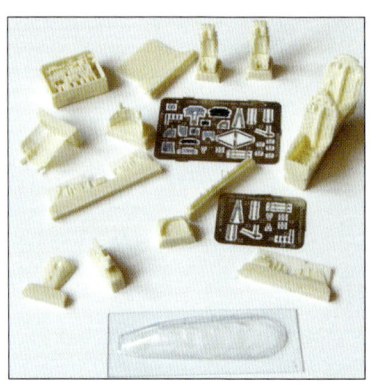

The contents of CMK's cockpit set

Pavla's set is simpler, but don't be deceived as it is every bit as good as the CMK set

Once painted the CMK cockpit is such an improvement on the kit parts that I'm lost for words

Resin cockpit, equipment bay, and front wheel bay are glued into place before the fuselage halves are joined together

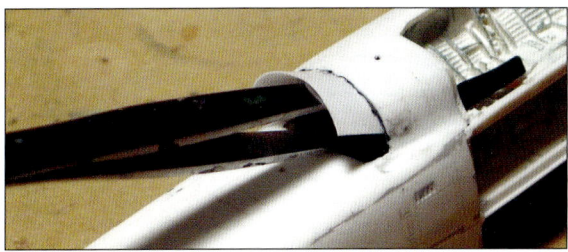

New intake trunking was simply made up from plastic card, and the end result was satisfactory

CMK's cockpit, once fitted, is worth all the effort it took to fit

Some firm clamping was required to close the fuselage around all that resin

detail their insides. I did like the Pavla seats, but sadly they would not fit the CMK tub without major work.

Once the fifteen resin parts were removed from the moulding blocks, they were hand painted, using Humbrol Steel Grey (87) as the main cockpit colour. This was given a black wash, then highlighted by dry-brushing. This done, the thirty-odd pre-painted etched items could be added, dealing with the instrument panels and the fittings on the two seats, embellishing the quality resin mouldings. All fitted well, until I came to dry fit the completed cockpit tub to the fuselage, and it became apparent that a lot of plastic and resin around this area would have to be removed to get the two fuselage halves to join together in the proper manner.

Before the cockpit was fitted, the panel for the resin electronics bay (just behind the cockpit on the right hand side) needed to be removed and the resin bay fitted from the inside. I also added the replacement front wheel bay, and then the fuselage halves could be joined together. Some trouble was experienced joining up the halves, and I was obliged to clamp things firmly, but even so a gap of 2mm remained on the top fuselage between the two cockpit sections, which was filled with plastic card. Interestingly the CMK canopies fitted with minimal adjustment.

With that out of the way, adding the new resin bomb/wheel bays to the inside of the fuselage was a breeze. The bay is a one-piece moulding and is one of the most stunning pieces of resin I've come across. I would love to know how they did it! Before the bay was fitted in place it was painted in satin white, with the raised detail highlighted with Steel Grey. Next on the menu are the four

replacement air brake housings. This required the removal of plastic around the air brake areas and the simple matter of gluing the CMK resin parts into place. When you come to do this, remember that the top sides of the lower housings should be flush with the fuselage!

Last of the major fuselage upgrades are the two engine intakes and relevant trunking. At first glance the CMK parts look very good and seem to offer a huge improvement on the stock parts, however when the inlets were offered up to the fuselage, it soon became apparent that something was very wrong, as the resin parts were way too small, and without some major reshaping of the fuselage would not fit. I resorted to using the Airfix intakes, scratch building inlet trunking and supplementary intake doors from plastic card.

With the exception of the canopies, exhausts and main wheels the rest of the kit was built from stock parts. CMK do supply some inserts for the flaps on the underside of the wing, but personally I don't feel they add enough to justify the work involved, as there is no interior detail, and in the end the only modification made to the wing was to thin down the rather thick trailing edge. With the wing added, the engine inlets could be glued into place and lashings of filler used to blend them in, and this was followed by the rudder. The new resin tailplanes were fitted after painting was completed, as was the engine exhaust assembly. Here CMK have hit the spot, with the simple exhausts being made up from three well-detailed parts that are direct replacements for the Airfix items, and easy to build, with a good fit to the kit's separate rear section of the fuselage.

On a bright note the undercarriage is one of the best aspects of the Airfix kit, being very well detailed, apart from the main wheels, and CMK supply a full set. The kit's wheel and bomb bay doors, as luck

91

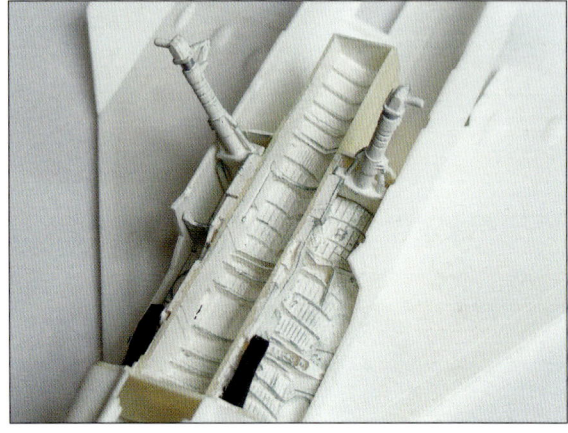

Painted and fitted into place, the main wheel/bomb bay, looks the part. The kit's undercarriage was used throughout the build

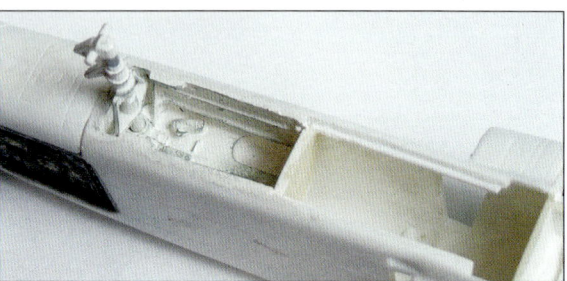

The front wheel bay, painted and fitted out with the kit's front undercarriage leg

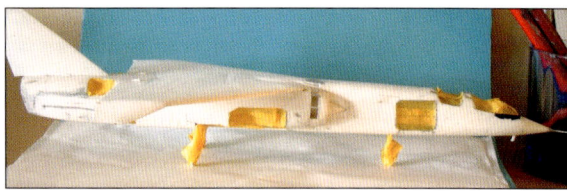

Taped up and ready for painting, my first time using an airbrush for such work

would have it, are acceptability detailed and were used instead of CMK's resin parts, as I made a right hash getting them off the moulding blocks.

After the painting it was canopy time, and anyone who has seen the Airfix kit will know these parts are not the kit's high spot, so vacforms are the order of the day, and are supplied in both the Pavla and CMK cockpit sets. CMK also provide resin inserts with interior detail and front framing for the opening sections, but sadly all the framing was broken beyond use, so just the rear inserts and some careful painting were utilized on the inside.

Two things not pointed out in either the Airfix or CMK

instructions are that the clear panels had an orange tint, and both of the canopies' clear sections had a black finish around them. Here a word of warning is required. The canopies were dipped in Klear as per usual, then Humbrol orange tint applied. The resulting reaction was a glutinous mass, and despite my best endeavours the damage was done and the tint ended up somewhat blotchy.

To round off the build the air brake assemblies, as well as all the bay doors, were fitted into place. Last of all, the separate rear section, complete with exhausts in place, was added along with the two resin tailplanes.

## Colour Options

The kit decals looked quite stunning, and cover three aircraft, XR219 (the only one to get off the ground), XR 220 and XR 222. All three have an anti-flash finish of all-over white. Airfix suggest a satin finish on all three aircraft, but my research points towards the satin for a factory fresh aircraft, a worn matt finish (and ample weathering) for XR 219, or a white gloss finish for XR 219/20 as they are preserved now in the UK. The decals are well printed, with a gloss film, and they all went on with no fuss at all. I did consider doing a 'What If?' finish, but in the end I feel that the TSR 2 looks its best in its original white. That said, Hannants do some very nice sheets in 1/72 and 1/48 so you can indulge yourself if the whim takes you with either Airfix kit, or with any other TSR 2 kit you may have at hand.

## Conclusion

It took some time for the aftermarket folks to get replacement parts out for this kit, but now there is a wide range of products available, from a simple pair of seats to all-inclusive packages. I have to say that even though I did not use all the parts in the packs, all of the CMK resin sets covered have something important to bring to the party, and with all that resin to hand, you can look forward to an enjoyable build, ending up with a really special model of a very charismatic and important aircraft.

# On Swing Wings of the Eagle

## Canadian Armed Forces CF-109

By Tony Grand

**TECH PANEL**

| | |
|---|---|
| BAC TSR 2 | |
| Scale: 1/72 | |
| Kit No: 07004 | |
| Type: Injection Moulded Plastic | |
| Manufacturer: Airfix | |

Having previously read up on the Avro CF-105 Arrow and its cancellation, I suppose I would inevitably be attracted to a what-if scenario in which its role was fulfilled, in the fullness of time, by an aircraft equally ill-fated in the real world, the TSR 2. So it was that I bought one of the Xtradecal sets including a 'Canadair CF-109', a licence-built TSR 2, modified for the long-range interceptor role and armed with four underwing AIM-54 Phoenix missiles plus an M-61 cannon in the bomb-bay replacing the CF-101 Voodoo. Xtradecal note that 'while ill-suited to the interceptor role the CF-109 worked reasonably well'.

'As well as a chocolate tea-pot' I thought on reading that, given that the TSR 2 was optimised for bombing the USSR's back yard by sneaking over the wall.

Paul Lucas, in his outstanding book *Lost Tomorrows of an Eagle*, sets out at length the evaluation of a possible interceptor TSR 2 carried out in 1963. The conclusion of the evaluation stated that, as it

existed, the TSR 2 would make a poor interceptor. The US - with the F-111 - had managed to combine the roles of low-level strike and interceptor aircraft in similar basic airframes by the use of different radar systems and variable geometry. As the TSR 2 was developed for low-level high-speed strike, it was thought to be unreasonable to expect it to perform these 'new' roles as well without undergoing a radical redesign, perhaps to the extent of invalidating the TSR 2 as it was then conceived. This does not mean that such development would not have been pursued, had TSR 2 survived, since the application of variable geometry had already been studied by Vickers (later a constituent of BAC) for some twenty years, and subsequent versions of the plane might well have benefited. There were, it seems, plans for a 'swing-wing' version of TSR 2 to emerge in the 1970s.

So, it was with this background that I started to consider what the Canadair CF-109 might have looked like. Clearly, a dedicated AI radar

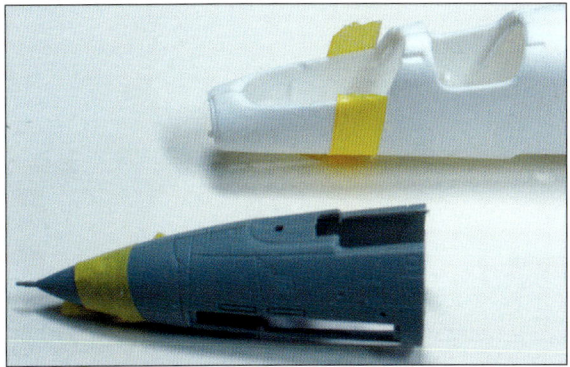

The nose transplant is about to begin – the Revell Tomcat meets the Airfix TSR.2 Unlikely bedfellows...

With a little test-fitting, fettling, and imagination, the front end can be made to work

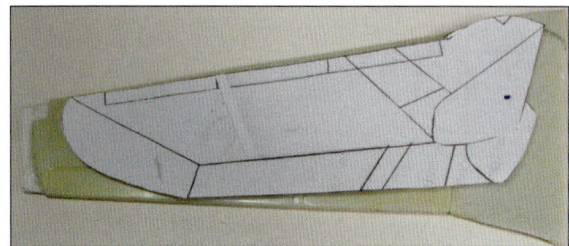

Template for wing glued to upper surface of spare Me 262 wing

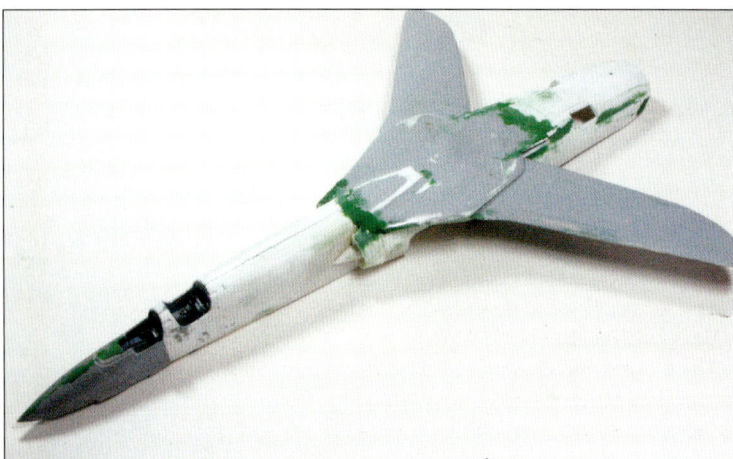

It'll be all right with a coat of paint...

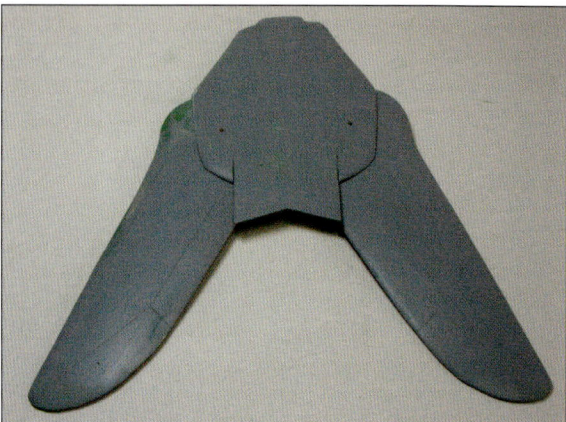

Upper surface of completed wing glove

Beginning to look promising

would be needed, as discussed at length in the study. Given that the Xtradecals are to adorn an aircraft in 1983, a dish of some 36 in diameter would be the order of the day, necessitating a larger, lengthened, nose. Again, by 1983, that Vickers/BAC research would have borne fruit, allowing the plane economical, long-range, high-altitude cruise or loiter on patrol, in addition to supersonic flight so it would act as a long-endurance combat air patrol fighter, to counter the threat posed by bombers. We might imagine that, with tanker support, the Combat Air Patrol (CAP) time might have been several hours.

## The Build

Swing wings, large nose: I obtained a Revell F-14D kit, to see what I could get from that. I knew the wings would be too small for my purposes but the swing mechanism might well come in handy, I hoped.

## The Nose

Having compared the kits, it seemed to me the F-14 nose could be made to blend in nicely with the TSR 2 fuselage. So, surgery began. There turned out to be a natural place to make the cut on both planes; immediately forward of the pilot's bulkhead. Having done that, I had to fettle both the TSR 2 fuselage and the F-14 nose, to get them to more or less the same width at the join. I cut a wedge out of the underside of the Tomcat's nose, then brought the cut edges together, using copious superglue to hold the joint. On the TSR 2 side, I packed out the joint with styrene shims, at top and bottom. Using the Tomcat nose had a further advantage: it had a port for the M61 cannon. I

reasoned that, with the introduction of miniaturised electronics, enough internal space would become available for the 'CF-109' to have that fit, rather than the suggested bomb-bay mounted item.

## The Fuselage

Apart from the necessary widening at the cockpit end, I reckoned the kit fuselage could remain much as it was. I did consider changing the intakes to the variable ramp kind but, noting that BAC studies had shown an advantage in the variable area, semi-circular, spiked type. I left them alone, although it remains open as to whether there would have been an advantage for a plane operating at high altitude rather than low. One for the aerodynamicists! I obtained the larger of the Eduard etches for the plane, containing detailing for the bomb-bay and main wheel-wells, reasoning that a couple of Phoenixes might well have been mounted in the bay. However, when I came to try this out, barely one missile could be fitted. Show an extra fuel tank fitted there? Not worth it, was my conclusion. So all that lovely detail is hidden. Think! as the *MAD* spoof of the IBM slogan used to say!

I also used the Pavla replacement cockpit tub and seats, but with

Most of this work will be covered up...

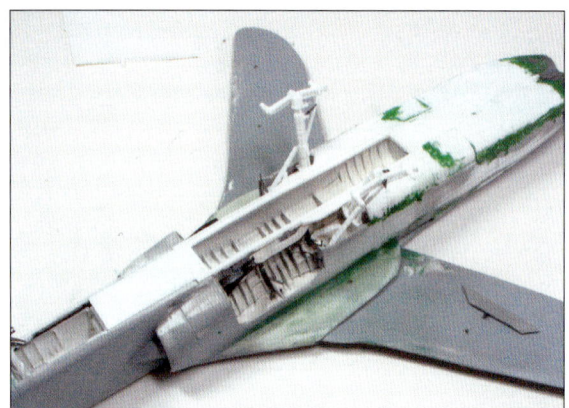

Canopies loosely in place. The front part is from the Revell Tomcat kit. Only the centre section had to be fabricated

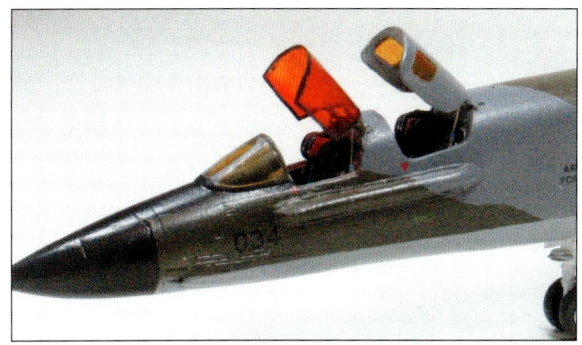

Completed canopies, showing increased visibility for pilot

The wing seal is made from masking tape. Rivets were added from an Archer sheet

the Eduard pre-painted instrument panels laid over the kit items (thus combining the best of the two) and a couple of their belts laid on top of the Pavla parts, as painting the Pavla detail is beyond me.

After closing up the fuselage, (first fitting the main u/c legs, as you can't do it afterwards) I fitted the air-brakes, closed, as they would seldom be open on the ground. This involved a lot of sanding and filling. All the fit issues will not be news to anyone who's built this kit!

## The Wings

Now, in Derek Wood's very well-known book, *Project Cancelled*, there appears a photo, showing part of a large poster display, captioned 'The BAC secret mini-exhibition at Warton in 1964 showed a variety of VG projects and conversions'. One of these, a plan view, is labelled ' TSR 2 Development'. It does not, however, match up with the plan view shown in *Lost Tomorrows of an Eagle*. Elucidation needed, so I contacted Paul Lucas, to ask what he knew. How helpful can a man be? Not only did Paul explain the discrepancy between the BAC poster and *Lost Tomorrows* but he sent me copies of the original drawings (upper and lower plan views) of the VG TSR 2 he had produced on the basis of the BAC poster. Gilt on the gingerbread: these showed conjectural pivot points for the wings and pylon positions.

Thus armed, I began the wings. There was a false start, as I had intended to modify the wing glove and pivot mechanism from the Tomcat. An attempt to do this resulted in a shoddy piece of scrap plastic and filler work which would I think have cracked open at some crucial point. Plan B involved modifying the kit's upper wing section to form the upper part of the glove and that worked well. Trim and fit, trim and fit…Those of a delicate disposition should turn away from the tale of cannibalism that follows. I didn't fancy building the swinging sections from laminated styrene, so I searched my kits for wings I could cannibalise. Which kit would I never build? The answer turned out to be the 1/32 Revell Me 262, a kit I've never seen a good word about. I glued the upper surface of each wing on to

a piece of thick styrene (to form the undersurface), then attached paper templates for the CF-109 wings. With a slitting saw and sanding drum on my Minicraft tool I made blanks, from which work with file and abrasives produced finished articles with plausible aerofoil sections. I used other sections from the Me 262 wings to make the underneath section of the glove.

Now to make those wings swing! Short lengths of brass wire were used as pivots and to couple the wings I used a strip of thin aluminium sheet, with pivot points arrived at by trial and much error. I had given up on using the 'gears' from the Tomcat, as there wouldn't be enough space within the wing. I used plastic rod for these pivots, as I could use a hot blade to form a kind of rivet. Having filled and primed the whole assembly a few times, I began cutting the appropriate areas of the fuselage away, to accept it: a short section behind the intakes; the whole of the support piece over the bomb-bay; and sections of the fuselage sides, to allow the movable sections to swing. A modicum of filler, scrap plastic and superglue later, the assembly was in place-and still working. One of the more fiddly bits was getting right the opening in the fuselage at the wing trailing edge.

As part of this stage, I also glued on the new nose and filled the gap between the fuselage halves created by widening the forward end. Much sanding and applications of Mr Surfacer later and the result looked reasonable. I also closed up the bomb-bay doors and those wheel-well doors, which only open whilst the u/c is cycling.

## The Cockpit Canopy

A combination of reasoning and aesthetics, this. I did consider going for the full bubble canopy, shown in *Lost Tomorrows* as proposed for the trainer version of the TSR 2, but that would have compromised the speed. I used the Tomcat windscreen, as it looked and fitted better, as well as providing better visibility. I was able to use the existing, replacement rear canopy section from the Pavla set, as I hadn't changed the opening for that, but I needed a new opening portion for

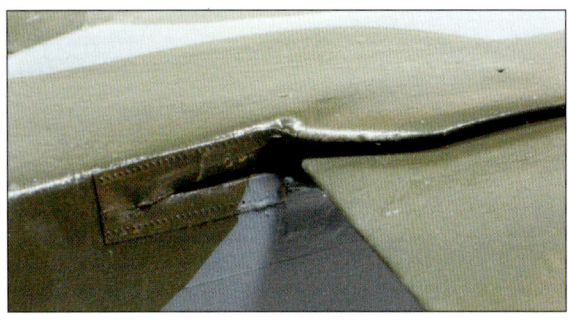

Archer's rivets are resin applied to decal film, and are a really useful innovation

the pilot. A balsa master was made, coated with Green Stuff for smoothness, and a replacement plug-moulded from packaging plastic. Not entirely logically, perhaps, I left the WSO with the same visibility as his navigator predecessor, but increased that of the pilot.

### The Pylons and Missiles

Paul Lucas had included on his plans, as well as hinge points and points for four pylons, conjectural outlines for ailerons, flaps and slats. This helped me to make the pylons the appropriate size to avoid fouling. I made two from thick pieces of styrene and modified two from those in the Tomcat kit. To make them pivot, I inserted a peg into each pylon and, at each attachment point on the wing, inserted a short length of aluminium tube. The pegs are a push fit and allow the pylons to be aligned as appropriate with the sweep of the wings. I calculated that as a Tornado GR 4 can carry four Sea Eagles, each weighing in at 580kg, on the swing portions of its wings, the CF-109 could cope with four 470 kg Phoenix AIMs. The missiles came from a Hasegawa weapons set.

### Refuelling and Pitot Probes

I made the housing for the refuelling probe from a length of sprue, flattened on one side, mounted on a piece of thin styrene. The pitot probe is a length of my dwindling supply of hypodermic tubing.

### Painting and Decaling

I followed the Xtradecal call-out for the paint-job: Canadian Light Grey 101-327 (FS363750) for the lower surfaces; upper surfaces Canadian Green 503-301 (approximates to FS34064) and Canadian Grey 501-302 (FS36118). FS34064 is described as Very Dark Drab on the indispensable Urban's Colour Reference Charts and I mixed it 50/50 from Mr Hobby H330 Dark Green (BS381C/641) and H304 Olive Drab (FS34087). I airbrushed on the two greys and brush-painted the green. The black radome, anti-dazzle and de-icing areas were brush-painted. The Xtradecal items went on extremely well over the usual coat of Klear.

I decided to retain the tinted canopies of the TSR 2 and

accordingly acquired some Humbrol 1322, Clear Orange. I started to brush this on, but as it is cellulose-based it dried very quickly and started to drag. So, I dipped the canopies in the tinlet, which worked well, except that it ended up rather dark. No danger of sunburn…

At this late stage (and I'm still not sure why I left it till this point) I simulated the inflatable seal at the wing trailing edge, by fitting two small lengths of masking tape and applying sections of Archer Fine Transfer rivets. You can coax the seals back into the closed position with a scalpel blade.

### Conclusion

I enjoyed this conversion. Doubtless, more lumps and bumps would qualify it better as a fighter of the era and I could have detailed it more, but I'm more satisfied with it than I would have been with applying the decals to an unmodified tactical bomber…

As a postscript, I've seen it said that we proposed an interceptor version of the TSR 2 to the Canadians, carrying Sparrow and Falcon air-to-air missiles, as a replacement for the cancelled Arrow. The Canadians didn't bite on the idea, which blessedly spared them the pain of being kicked in the teeth twice.

### References:

- *Project Cancelled*, Derek Wood, revised edition, Jane's 1986
- *TSR-2: Phoenix or Folly?* Frank Barnett-Jones, GMS Enterprises 1994
- *Lost Tomorrows of an Eagle*, Paul Lucas, SAM Publications 2009
- British Aircraft Corporation TSR 2, Anthony Thornborough, Ad Hoc Publications 2005
- *British Secret Projects: Jet Bombers since 1949*, Tony Buttler, Midland 2003
- *British Secret Projects: Jet Fighters since 1950*, Tony Buttler, Midland 2000

# Testing Time

### Airfix's 1/48 TSR 2 Test Shot

By David Francis

I will not bore you with a history of the TSR 2 as there are many books on the subject that can do a better job than me. In model form there had been quite a few limited run and vacform kits produced thenAirfix produced a mainstream 1/72 kit, and as it was a fairly limited run it rapidly disappeared from hobby shop shelves, only to reappear on eBay, in many cases at vastly inflated prices. Obviously a financial success, we now have the big brother but one thing I will make clear is that this is not just a scale up of the smaller kit.

On inspection of the sprues it is apparent the engraved detail in the cockpit and undercarriage bays is the equal of anything from Japan. The engraved panel lines are a bit overdone, not quite trench-like but not as fine as other kits, and some of the panel lines are not complete, although bear in mind again, this is a test shot so this may not be the case on a production model. The next thing I noticed were some pin marks in between the detail in the undercarriage bays and some large sink marks on the fuselage adjacent to the locating lugs. At first this had me quite worried as I hate trying to fill pin marks, especially when they lie between moulded detail, then I realised that this kit was really well engineered as all of these sink and pin marks were hidden behind panels or separate duct work.

**TECH PANEL**

| | |
|---|---|
| Scale: | 1/48 |
| Kit No: | 10105 |
| Status: | New Tooling |
| Type: | Injection Moulded plastic |
| Manufacturer: | Airfix |

## Construction

Construction started with the cockpit and this is quite nice, especially on the bulkheads. The ejector seats are also very good and just need brass seatbelts added to look quite acceptable. As in the recent Canberra kits we have lots of nice detail but in one of the most obvious areas – the instrument panels – there is virtually nothing, so as I was building a 'What If' I added some of Eduard's pre-painted etched brass, designed for a Vigilante, to my model.

To be fair to Airfix I am sure the aftermarket will soon produce dedicated sets to add the missing detail, and unless you leave the canopy open you can see virtually nothing in the cockpit as the windows are quite small.

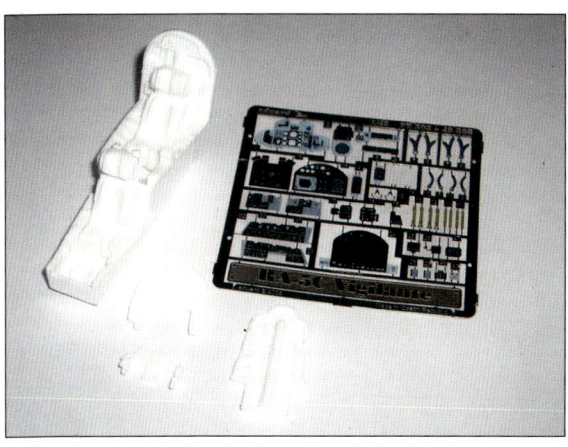

The basic cockpit is well detailed but some Eduard brass added more to the instrument panels

Nothing can compare to Eduard pre-coloured brass for a quick fix to a cockpit

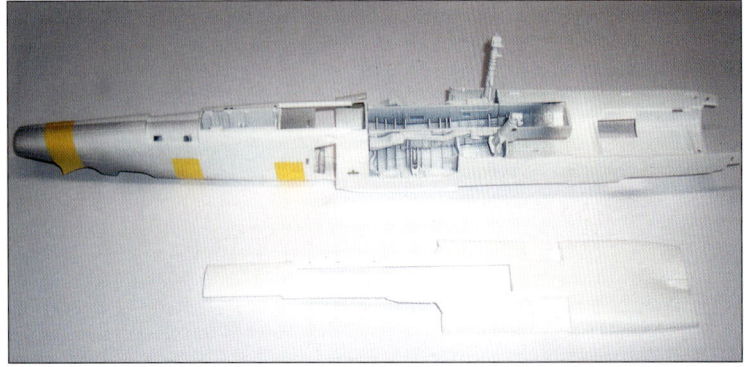

Here you can see the way that the separate panels are used to hide any sink marks

Only small amounts of filler were needed but I hated the white plastic which made it hard to see if the joint was perfect

The undercarriage bays are very well detailed but on the TSR 2 the large doors are closed unless the undercarriage is retracting or undergoing maintenance, so most of this will be hidden on the finished model. The undercarriage legs are very solid, much like the original, which was designed to operate from unprepared runways. Certainly some parts are over scale, like the trailing links, but again I am sure aftermarket replacements will be available shortly after the kit arrives. To finish the undercarriage you have the wheels, and these have a weighted effect that is a bit overdone but looks better than a model resting on the tips of its toes. The main bomb bays also show a good level of detail and you are supplied with a choice of an atomic weapon or fuel tanks to fill it.

With all the fiddly bits done I now assembled the rest of the kit, and there are only two areas that needed a little TLC. The first is the intakes, the fit of which can be improved with some careful sanding and test fitting, and the second is the wing-to-fuselage join. On my example the rear of the wing sat a little low in its cutout, but by adding a small Plasticard shim under the rear section of the wing I raised it enough to produce a seamless smooth joint.

With all the main assembly done I decided to add a few details, some spurious and some that are not. First off were intakes and scoops. The TSR 2 has a few of these around the rear fuselage and Airfix have moulded them as solid lumps and as I did not fancy hollowing them out I replaced them with some similar looking ones from a Quickboost MiG-19 intake set. As I wanted to produce a production TSR 2 I added a few extra scoops from this set around the undersides and on the fuselage sides, and even added a pod under the nose from Hasegawa's Draken kit to represent a FLIR system.

I also raided Revell's Eurofighter Typhoon for some stores, as this kit includes a massive selection. I added underwing fuel tanks and a set of pylons using the mounting points engraved on the wings to aid positioning.

The construction of this kit took just over a week and was a pleasure from start to finish, but now I had to find a colour scheme that could be painted over a weekend as the deadline for this issue was fast approaching.

## Painting and Decalling

I had the three sheets that Hannants have produced offering What If schemes for the TSR 2, and I was tempted by one in Raspberry Ripple or the NASA example, but these were not weekend paint jobs, requiring some careful masking and difficult colours like white and orange. Instead I was drawn to an Australian scheme, but then I remembered a sheet that Aussie Decals had produced for the F-111 with a striking Number One and a Kookaburra on the tail that would look good on the TSR 2 fin. Even better, current Aussie F-111s are finished in an overall dark grey scheme.

As is my habit I first gave the model an overall coat of Halfords black primer, which revealed a few seams that needed a little more work, as well as acting as a pre-shading for the top colour. I used Tamiya German Grey acrylic for my main colour thinned 60/40 with their own thinners, and started by applying solid colour to the centre of panels before misting lighter coats over the panel lines to add a little variation to the one-colour scheme.

After decalling I did a little touching up with a small brush before applying a little weathering with pastel powders and Pro Modeller washes.

## Conclusion

Obviously I cannot comment on the instructions and decals as I did not have any, but the basic kit is very good, with just enough detail for a nice out-of-the-box build at a reasonable price, but with plenty of areas that the aftermarket boys can step into and improve on for those who really want to go to town. Though the original white colour scheme may be essential for the purist I am sure we will see many like mine in What If schemes on club stands in 2009.

The impressive tail art from an Aussie Decals sheet